Python for Web APIs

Design, Build, and Integrate RESTful APIs

Derek Randolph

2

3

Disclaimer

The information contained in this book, *Python for Web APIs: Design, Build, and Integrate RESTful APIs*, is provided for educational and informational purposes only. The content within these pages is intended to assist readers in understanding the principles of designing, building, and integrating RESTful APIs using Python.

While every effort has been made to ensure the accuracy and completeness of the information provided, the author, Derek Randolph, and any associated parties make no guarantees regarding the accuracy, reliability, or suitability of the content. The information is presented "as-is" and may not reflect the most current developments or practices in the field of web development and API design.

Introduction

Welcome to **"Python for Web APIs: Design, Build, and Integrate RESTful APIs"**—your gateway to mastering the art of creating powerful, efficient, and secure web APIs with Python.

In today's digital age, web APIs are the backbone of modern web applications, driving interactions and powering integrations across diverse platforms. Whether you're a seasoned developer or just starting your journey into the world of web development, understanding how to design, build, and integrate RESTful APIs is essential. This ebook is your comprehensive guide to unlocking the full potential of Python in the realm of web APIs.

Python stands out as a versatile, powerful language that simplifies complex tasks and accelerates development. Its rich ecosystem of libraries and frameworks, coupled with its clean, readable syntax, makes it the ideal choice for building and integrating web APIs. From small projects to large-scale applications, Python offers the tools and flexibility you need to create robust solutions.

This ebook is crafted to provide you with a step-by-step approach to mastering web APIs using Python. Here's what awaits you:

Learn the principles of designing RESTful APIs that are both user-friendly and scalable. We'll delve into best practices for defining endpoints, structuring responses, and managing data.

Get hands-on with Python frameworks like Flask and FastAPI, which will help you construct APIs efficiently. We'll cover everything from setting up your development environment to implementing authentication and handling different HTTP methods.

Discover how to seamlessly integrate your APIs with web applications. Explore real-world examples and techniques for ensuring smooth communication between your front-end and back-end systems.

Security is paramount in today's web landscape. We'll guide you through best practices for securing your APIs against common vulnerabilities, ensuring your data and user interactions remain safe.

As technology evolves, so do API practices. We'll touch upon advanced topics and emerging trends in API development, preparing you for the future of web technologies.

Chapter 1: Python for Web APIs

The use of web APIs has become increasingly popular for developers looking to access and interact with data from various online sources. Python, a versatile and powerful programming language, has emerged as a popular choice for building web APIs due to its simplicity, readability, and extensive library support.

This chapter will serve as an introduction to Python web APIs, providing an overview of what they are, how they work, and why they are important in the world of web development. We will explore the basics of working with web APIs using Python, including how to make requests, handle responses, and parse data.

What is a Web API?

A web API, or Application Programming Interface, is a set of rules and protocols that allow different software applications to communicate with each other over the internet. Web APIs are used to access and interact with data from online services, such as social media platforms, e-commerce websites, and weather services.

Web APIs are typically accessed using HTTP requests, which allow developers to retrieve data from a server and perform various operations on that data. APIs can return data in a variety of formats, such as JSON or XML, which can then be processed and displayed in a web application.

9

Python and Web APIs

Python is a versatile and powerful programming language that is well-suited for working with web APIs. Python's simplicity and readability make it easy for developers to quickly build and deploy web API clients, while its extensive library support provides tools for handling HTTP requests, parsing data, and interacting with web services.

Python's requests library, for example, provides a simple and intuitive interface for making HTTP requests to web APIs. With just a few lines of code, developers can retrieve data from a web API, handle responses, and extract the information they need for their applications.

Working with Web APIs in Python

To demonstrate how to work with web APIs in Python, let's consider a simple example using the OpenWeatherMap API. The OpenWeatherMap API provides weather data for cities around the world, allowing developers to retrieve information such as current weather conditions, temperature, and humidity.

To access the OpenWeatherMap API in Python, we first need to install the requests library using pip:

```
pip install requests
```

Next, we can write a Python script to make a request to the

OpenWeatherMap API and retrieve weather data for a specific city. Here is an example script that retrieves the current weather conditions for New York City:

```python
import requests

api_key = 'YOUR_API_KEY'
city = 'New York'
url = f'http://api.openweathermap.org/data/2.5/weather?q={city}&appid={api_key}'

response = requests.get(url)
data = response.json()

print(f'Current weather in {city}: {data["weather"][0]["description"]}')
print(f'Temperature: {data["main"]["temp"]}°C')
print(f'Humidity: {data["main"]["humidity"]}%')
```

In this script, we first define our API key and the city we want to retrieve weather data for. We then construct the URL for the API request, including the city name and API key. We use the requests.get() method to make a GET request to the API, and then use the response.json() method to parse the JSON data returned by the API.

Finally, we extract and print the current weather conditions, temperature, and humidity for the specified city. This example demonstrates how easy it is to work with web APIs in Python using the requests library.

We have introduced the concept of web APIs and explored

how Python can be used to interact with them. We have seen how Python's simplicity and readability make it well-suited for working with web APIs, and how libraries such as requests provide tools for making HTTP requests and handling responses.

In the following chapters, we will delve deeper into working with web APIs in Python, exploring topics such as authentication, error handling, and data manipulation. By the end of this book, you will have a solid understanding of how to build and consume web APIs using Python, and be ready to tackle more advanced projects in web development.

Understanding RESTful Architecture

RESTful architecture is a key concept in modern web development that allows for the creation of scalable, flexible, and efficient web services. Understanding RESTful architecture is essential for any developer looking to build successful web applications. In this article, we will explore the fundamentals of RESTful architecture, its key principles, and how it can be implemented in practice.

What is RESTful architecture?

RESTful architecture, or Representational State Transfer, is a style of software architecture that defines a set of constraints for creating web services. These constraints are designed to make web services more scalable, flexible, and efficient by defining a uniform interface for interacting with resources.

At its core, RESTful architecture is based on the concept of resources, which are identified by unique URLs. These resources can represent any type of data, such as user profiles, products, or orders. Clients can interact with these resources using standard HTTP methods, such as GET, POST, PUT, and DELETE.

Key principles of RESTful architecture

RESTful architecture is based on a set of key principles that define how web services should be designed and implemented. These principles include:

Client-server architecture: RESTful services are based on a client-server architecture, where clients and servers are separate entities that communicate over a network. This separation of concerns allows for greater flexibility and scalability in web services.

Statelessness: RESTful services are stateless, meaning that each request from a client to a server is independent and self-contained. This allows for greater reliability and scalability in web services, as servers do not need to maintain client state between requests.

Uniform interface: RESTful services use a uniform interface for interacting with resources, which is based on standard HTTP methods. This allows for greater interoperability between clients and servers, as well as easier maintenance and evolution of web services.

Resource identification: Resources in RESTful services are identified by unique URLs, which are used to access and manipulate the resource. This allows for greater flexibility and scalability in web services, as resources can be easily located and accessed by clients.

Representation: Resources in RESTful services are represented in a standard format, such as JSON or XML. This allows for greater flexibility and interoperability in web services, as clients can easily parse and understand the data returned by a server.

The power of Python in Web APIs

Python has become one of the most popular programming languages in recent years, and for good reason. With its simple syntax, readability, and versatility, Python has found its way into a wide range of applications, including web development. In particular, Python has become a powerful tool for creating web APIs, which are essential for modern web applications.

Web APIs, or Application Programming Interfaces, allow different software applications to communicate with each other over the internet. They provide a way for developers to access and interact with web services, such as databases, servers, and other online resources. Web APIs are essential for building dynamic and interactive web applications, and Python's flexibility and ease of use make it an ideal choice for creating them.

One of the key reasons why Python is so well-suited for web APIs is its extensive library support. Python has a vast ecosystem of libraries and frameworks that make it easy to build and deploy web APIs quickly and efficiently. Some of the most popular libraries for creating web APIs in Python include Flask, Django, and FastAPI.

Flask is a lightweight and flexible web framework that is perfect for building simple web APIs. With Flask, developers can quickly create routes and endpoints for their API, as well as handle requests and responses. Flask is easy to learn and use, making it a great choice for

15

beginners and experienced developers alike.

Django, on the other hand, is a more robust web framework that is ideal for building complex web APIs. Django provides a full-featured set of tools for building web applications, including authentication, database management, and security features. While Django has a steeper learning curve than Flask, it offers more functionality and scalability for larger projects.

FastAPI is a newer web framework that has gained popularity for its speed and performance. FastAPI is built on top of the Starlette ASGI framework and provides a simple and intuitive way to create web APIs. With its automatic data validation and serialization features, FastAPI makes it easy to build robust and efficient APIs.

In addition to these frameworks, Python also has a number of libraries that make it easy to work with web APIs. The requests library, for example, provides a simple and intuitive way to make HTTP requests and handle responses. With requests, developers can easily send GET, POST, PUT, and DELETE requests to web APIs, as well as handle authentication and error handling.

Another popular library for working with web APIs in Python is the json library, which makes it easy to serialize and deserialize JSON data. Many web APIs use JSON as their data format, so the json library is essential for parsing and manipulating API responses. With the json library, developers can easily convert Python objects to JSON strings and vice versa, making it simple to work with API data in their applications.

Python's versatility and ease of use make it a powerful tool for creating web APIs, but its real power lies in its ability to integrate with other technologies. Python can easily interact with databases, servers, and other web services, making it easy to build dynamic and interactive web applications. With Python, developers can create APIs that fetch data from external sources, process it, and return it to the client in a format that is easy to work with.

One of the key advantages of using Python for web APIs is its strong community support. The Python community is large and active, with a wealth of resources and tutorials available for developers of all skill levels. Whether you are a beginner or an experienced developer, you can find support and guidance from the Python community to help you build and deploy web APIs.

Another advantage of using Python for web APIs is its scalability. Python's simplicity and readability make it easy to build and maintain large-scale web applications. With Python, developers can easily scale their APIs to handle high volumes of traffic and large amounts of data. Python's asynchronous programming features, such as asyncio and aiohttp, make it easy to build high-performance web APIs that can handle multiple requests concurrently.

In addition to its scalability, Python also offers strong security features for web APIs. Python's built-in security features, such as its standard library modules for encryption and hashing, make it easy to secure API endpoints and protect sensitive data. With Python, developers can implement authentication and authorization mechanismsto ensure that only authorized users can access their APIs.

Overall, the power of Python in web APIs lies in its simplicity, versatility, and scalability. With its extensive library support, strong community, and security features, Python is an ideal choice for building dynamic and interactive web applications. Whether you are a beginner or an experienced developer, Python provides the toolsand resources you need to create powerful web APIs that can handle a wide range of tasks and data sources.

In conclusion, Python's power in web APIs is undeniable. With its simplicity, versatility, and scalability, Python has become a go-to language for building web APIs that are fast, efficient, and secure. Whether you are building a simple REST API or a complex microservices architecture, Python provides the tools and resources you needto create

Chapter 2: Advantages of RESTful APIs

In the world of software development, RESTful APIs have become increasingly popular due to their numerous advantages. In this chapter, we will explore some of the key benefits of using RESTful APIs in language.

Simplicity and ease of use
One of the main advantages of RESTful APIs is their simplicity and ease of use. RESTful APIs are based on a set of well-defined principles that make them easy to understand and implement. This simplicity makes it easier for developers to work with RESTful APIs, reducing the time and effort required to integrate them into their applications.

Scalability
RESTful APIs are highly scalable, allowing developers to easily add new features and functionality to their applications without having to make significant changes to the existing codebase. This scalability is particularly important in language, where applications often need to support a large number of users and handle a high volume of requests.

Flexibility
RESTful APIs are highly flexible, allowing developers to easily customize and extend them to meet the specific needs of their applications. This flexibility makes it easier

for developers to create APIs that are tailored to their unique requirements, rather than being limited by the constraints of a pre-defined interface.

Performance
RESTful APIs are known for their high performance, as they are designed to be lightweight and efficient. This performance is particularly important in language, where applications often need to process large amounts of data and handle complex operations in real-time. By using RESTful APIs, developers can ensure that their applications are able to deliver the performance and responsiveness that users expect.

Security
RESTful APIs are inherently secure, as they use standard HTTP methods and protocols to communicate between clients and servers. This security is particularly important in language, where applications often handle sensitive data and need to protect against potential security threats. By using RESTful APIs, developers can ensure that their applications are secure and protected from unauthorized access.

Compatibility
RESTful APIs are highly compatible with a wide range of programming languages, frameworks, and platforms. This compatibility makes it easier for developers to integrate RESTful APIs into their applications, regardless of the technology stack they are using. This interoperability is particularly important in language, where applications often need to communicate with a variety of external systems and services.

Documentation

RESTful APIs are well-documented, making it easy for developers to understand how they work and how to use them in their applications. This documentation includes detailed descriptions of the API endpoints, parameters, and response formats, as well as examples and code snippets to help developers get started quickly. This documentation is particularly important in language, where applications often need to be able to communicate with external systems and services.

RESTful APIs offer a wide range of advantages for developers working in language. From their simplicity and ease of use to their scalability, flexibility, performance, security, compatibility, and documentation, RESTful APIs provide a powerful and efficient way to build and integrate APIs into applications. By leveraging the benefits of RESTful APIs, developers can create robust and reliable applications that meet the needs of users and deliver a seamless user experience.

HTTP Methods and Status Codes

HTTP Methods and Status Codes are essential components of the Hypertext Transfer Protocol (HTTP) used for communication between clients and servers on the World Wide Web. Understanding these methods and status codes is crucial for web developers and network administrators to effectively manage and troubleshoot web applications. In this article, we will explore the most common HTTP methods and status codes and their significance in web development.

HTTP Methods:

HTTP defines several methods or verbs that specify the action to be performed on a resource identified by a URL. Each method has a specific purpose and behavior, and they are used to perform different operations on the server. The most commonly used HTTP methods are:

GET: The GET method is used to retrieve data from a server. It is a safe and idempotent method, meaning that it should not have any side effects on the server and can be called multiple times without changing the server's state.

POST: The POST method is used to submit data to a server to create a new resource. It is not idempotent, meaning that multiple calls to the same URL with the same data may result in different outcomes.

PUT: The PUT method is used to update or replace an

existing resource on the server. It is idempotent,meaning that multiple calls to the same URL with the same data will have the same effect.

DELETE: The DELETE method is used to remove a resource from the server. It is idempotent, meaning that multiple calls to the same URL will have the same effect.

PATCH: The PATCH method is used to partially update a resource on the server. It is not idempotent,meaning that multiple calls to the same URL with the same data may result in different outcomes.

HEAD: The HEAD method is similar to the GET method, but it only retrieves the headers of a resource without the body. It is useful for checking the status of a resource without downloading its entire content.

OPTIONS: The OPTIONS method is used to retrieve information about the communication options availablefor a resource or server. It is often used to determine the supported methods and headers for a given resource.

TRACE: The TRACE method is used to echo the received request back to the client. It is primarily used for diagnostic purposes to test and debug the communication between the client and server.

HTTP Status Codes:

HTTP status codes are three-digit numbers that indicate the outcome of an HTTP request. They are divided intofive categories based on their first digit:

Informational (1xx): These status codes indicate that the server has received the request and is processing it.They are used to provide feedback to the client about the status of the request.

Success (2xx): These status codes indicate that the request was successful and the server has fulfilled it. The most common success status code is 200 (OK), which indicates that the request was successful.

Redirection (3xx): These status codes indicate that the client must take additional action to complete the request. They are used to redirect the client to a different URL or resource.

Client Error (4xx): These status codes indicate that there was an error in the client's request. The most common client error status code is 404 (Not Found), which indicates that the requested resource could not be found on the server.

Server Error (5xx): These status codes indicate that there was an error on the server while processing the request. The most common server error status code is 500 (Internal Server Error), which indicates a generic server error.

Some of the most common HTTP status codes are:

200 (OK): The request was successful.
201 (Created): The request has been fulfilled and a new

resource has been created.

204 (No Content): The server has fulfilled the request but there is no content to send back.

301 (Moved Permanently): The requested resource has been permanently moved to a new location.

400 (Bad Request): The server could not understand the request due to invalid syntax.

401 (Unauthorized): The client must authenticate itself to get access to the requested resource.

403 (Forbidden): The client does not have permission to access the requested resource.

404 (Not Found): The requested resource could not be found on the server.

500 (Internal Server Error): A generic server error occurred while processing the request.

HTTP methods and status codes play a crucial role in the communication between clients and servers on the web. By understanding these methods and status codes, web developers and network administrators can effectively manage and troubleshoot web applications. It is important to use the appropriate HTTP method for each operation and handle the corresponding status codes to provide a seamless user experience.

HTTP methods and status codes are fundamental concepts in web development that govern the interaction between clients and servers.

RESTful API Design Principles

RESTful API design principles are essential for creating efficient and user-friendly APIs that adhere to industry standards and best practices. By following these principles, developers can ensure that their APIs are scalable, maintainable, and easy to use. In this article, we will discuss some of the key RESTful API design principles and how they can be applied in practice.

Use HTTP methods effectively

One of the fundamental principles of RESTful API design is to use HTTP methods effectively. HTTP provides a set of methods that can be used to perform different actions on resources, such as GET, POST, PUT, DELETE, etc. When designing an API, it is important to use these methods in a consistent and meaningful way.

For example, GET should be used to retrieve information about a resource, POST should be used to create a new resource, PUT should be used to update an existing resource, and DELETE should be used to delete a resource. By using these methods consistently, developers can create APIs that are intuitive and easy to understand.

Use resource-oriented URLs

Another important principle of RESTful API design is to use resource-oriented URLs. In RESTful APIs, resources are represented by URLs, and each resource should have

26

its own unique URL. By using resource-oriented URLs, developers can create APIs that are self-descriptive and easy to navigate.

For example, instead of using URLs like /getUsers or /updateUser, developers should use URLs like /users to represent a collection of users and /users/{id} to represent a specific user. By using resource-oriented URLs, developers can create APIs that are more intuitive and easier to work with.

Use meaningful status codes

Status codes are an important part of any API, as they provide information about the outcome of a request. When designing a RESTful API, it is important to use meaningful status codes that accurately reflect the result of a request.

For example, a successful GET request should return a 200 status code, while a request that results in a resource not found should return a 404 status code. By using meaningful status codes, developers can create APIs that are easier to troubleshoot and debug.

Use hypermedia

Hypermedia is a key concept in RESTful API design that involves including links to related resources in API responses. By including hypermedia links in API responses, developers can create APIs that are more discoverable and easier to navigate.

For example, a response to a GET request for a user resource could include links to related resources, such as the user's profile or a list of the user's friends. By including hypermedia links in API responses, developers can create APIs that are more flexible and easier to work with.

Use versioning

Versioning is an important aspect of API design that involves specifying the version of the API in the URL. By using versioning, developers can ensure that clients can continue to use the API even as it evolves over time.

For example, instead of using URLs like /users, developers should use URLs like /v1/users to specify the version of the API. By using versioning, developers can create APIs that are more stable and easier to maintain.

Use authentication and authorization

Authentication and authorization are essential for securing APIs and ensuring that only authorized users can access sensitive resources. When designing a RESTful API, it is important to implement authentication and authorization mechanisms that are robust and secure.

For example, developers can use OAuth 2.0 for authentication and authorization, which allows clients to obtain access tokens that can be used to access protected resources. By using authentication and authorization, developers can create APIs that are more secure and reliable.

Use pagination

Pagination is an important concept in API design that involves breaking up large sets of data into smaller chunks to improve performance and reduce the load on servers. When designing a RESTful API, it is important to implement pagination mechanisms that allow clients to retrieve data in manageable chunks.

For example, developers can use query parameters like ?page=1&limit=10 to specify the page number and the number of items per page. By using pagination, developers can create APIs that are more efficient and scalable.

Use error handling

Error handling is an important aspect of API design that involves providing meaningful error messages to clients when something goes wrong. When designing a RESTful API, it is important to implement error handling mechanisms that provide detailed information about the cause of an error.

For example, a request that results in a server error should return a 500 status code along with an error message that explains what went wrong. By using error handling, developers can create APIs that are more user-friendly and easier to work with.

In conclusion, RESTful API design principles are essential for creating efficient and user-friendly APIs that adhere to industry standards and best practices. By following these principles, developers can ensure that their APIs are scalable, maintainable, and easy to use.

Chapter 3: Introduction to HTTP and REST

We will delve into the fundamental concepts of HTTP and REST, two crucial technologies that form the backbone of modern web development. Understanding these concepts is essential for any developer looking to build robust and scalable web applications.

HTTP, or Hypertext Transfer Protocol, is the foundation of data communication on the World Wide Web. It is a protocol that allows web browsers and servers to communicate with each other by sending and receiving data.
HTTP operates on a client-server model, where a client, typically a web browser, sends a request to a server, which then processes the request and sends back a response.

The basic structure of an HTTP request consists of a method, a URL, headers, and a body. The method specifies the action to be performed, such as GET, POST, PUT, or DELETE. The URL identifies the resource being requested or manipulated. Headers provide additional information about the request, such as the content type or authentication credentials. The body contains the data being sent to the server, such as form data or JSON payload.

HTTP responses also follow a similar structure, with a status code indicating the outcome of the request, headers providing additional information, and a body containing the response data. Status codes range from 1xx for informational responses to 5xx for server errors, with the most common ones being 2xx for successful requests and 4xx for client errors.

REST, or Representational State Transfer, is a set of architectural principles for designing networked applications. RESTful APIs, which adhere to these principles, use HTTP methods to perform CRUD (Create, Read, Update, Delete) operations on resources. This makes REST a powerful and flexible approach for building web services that can be easily consumed by clients.

One of the key principles of REST is the concept of resources, which are identified by unique URLs. These resources can be manipulated using standard HTTP methods, such as GET for retrieving data, POST for creating new resources, PUT for updating existing resources, and DELETE for removing resources. By following these conventions, RESTful APIs provide a consistent and intuitive interface for interacting with web services.

Another important concept in REST is statelessness, which means that each request from a client to a server contains all the information necessary to process the request. This simplifies server-side logic and improves scalability, as servers do not need to maintain session state between requests. Instead, clients can include authentication tokens or other credentials in each request to identify themselves.

RESTful APIs also make use of hypermedia, which allows clients to navigate through resources by following links embedded in responses. This enables a more dynamic and discoverable API design, where clients can explore available actions and resources without prior knowledge of the API structure.

In this chapter, we will explore how to design and implement RESTful APIs using HTTP methods and status codes. We will also discuss best practices for resource naming, versioning, and error handling. By mastering these concepts, you will be well-equipped to build scalable and maintainable web applications that leverage the power of HTTP and REST.

Resources and Representations in APIs

APIs, or Application Programming Interfaces, are a crucial component of modern software development. They allow different software systems to communicate with each other, enabling developers to access and use the functionality of other applications in their own projects. In order to effectively work with APIs, developers need to understand the concepts of resources and representations.

Resources are the fundamental building blocks of APIs. They represent the data or functionality that an API exposes to the outside world. For example, a social media API might have resources such as users, posts, and comments. Each resource has a unique identifier, which allows clients to access and manipulate it through the API.

Representations, on the other hand, are the different ways in which resources can be presented to clients. Representations can take many forms, such as JSON, XML, or HTML. When a client makes a request to an API for a resource, the API responds with a representation of that resource in the requested format.

One of the key principles of APIs is the separation of concerns between resources and representations. This means that the API should expose resources independently of how they are represented. For example, a client should be able to request a user resource in JSON format, XML format, or any other format that the API supports, without affecting the underlying user resource itself.

In order to work effectively with APIs, developers need to understand how resources and representations are defined and managed. This involves defining the structure and properties of resources, as well as specifying how they can be accessed and manipulated through the API. Developers also need to consider how different representations of resources can be generated and consumed by clients.

There are several common approaches to defining resources and representations in APIs. One popular approach is to use REST, or Representational State Transfer, which is a set of architectural principles for designing networked applications. In a RESTful API, resources are typically represented as URLs, and different representations of those resources are accessed through HTTP methods such as GET, POST, PUT, and DELETE.

Another approach is to use GraphQL, which is a query language for APIs that allows clients to request specific data from a server. With GraphQL, clients can define the structure of the data they need, and the server responds with a JSON representation of that data. This approach gives clients more flexibility and control over the data they receive from the API.

In addition to defining resources and representations, developers also need to consider how to handle errors and exceptions in APIs. When a client makes a request to an API, there is always the possibility that something could go wrong, such as a resource not being found or an invalid request being made. APIs need to provide clear and informative error messages to clients, so that they can understand what went wrong and how to correct it.

Resources and representations are essential concepts in API development. By understanding how resources are defined and managed, and how different representations of those resources are generated and consumed, developers can create robust and flexible APIs that meet the needs of their clients. By following best practices and principles such as REST and GraphQL, developers can ensure that their APIs are well-designed, easy to use, and reliable.

Choosing the Right Tools with python for APIs

When it comes to building APIs in Python, choosing the right tools is crucial for creating efficient and scalable applications. In this article, we will discuss the importance of selecting the right tools for building APIs in Python and provide a guide on how to choose the best tools for your project.

Why Choosing the Right Tools is Important

Choosing the right tools for building APIs in Python is essential for several reasons. First and foremost, the tools you use can greatly impact the performance, scalability, and security of your API. By selecting the right tools, you can ensure that your API is fast, reliable, and secure, which will ultimately lead to a better user experience.

Additionally, choosing the right tools can also save you time and effort in the long run. By using tools that are well-documented, well-supported, and easy to use, you can streamline the development process and avoid common pitfalls and roadblocks. This can help you deliver your API faster and with fewer bugs, ultimately saving you time and resources.

Furthermore, choosing the right tools can also help you future-proof your API. By selecting tools that are widely used and well-maintained, you can ensure that your API will be compatible with future updates and changes to the Python language and its ecosystem. This can help you avoid having to rewrite large portions of your codebase in the future, saving you time and effort down the line.

How to Choose the Right Tools for Building APIs in Python

When it comes to choosing the right tools for building APIs in Python, there are several factors to consider. Here are some key considerations to keep in mind when selecting tools for your project:

Functionality: The first thing to consider when choosing tools for building APIs in Python is the functionality they provide. Make sure that the tools you select offer all the features and capabilities you need to build your API. This includes support for common API protocols and standards, such as REST, GraphQL, and SOAP, as well as features like authentication, rate limiting, and error handling.

Performance: Another important factor to consider is the performance of the tools you choose. Make sure that the tools you select are fast and efficient, as this will directly impact the speed and responsiveness of your API. Look for tools that are optimized for performance and can handle a high volume of requests without slowing down or crashing.

Scalability: Scalability is another crucial consideration when choosing tools for building APIs in Python. Make sure that the tools you select can scale with your API as it grows in size and complexity. Look for tools that are designed to handle large amounts of traffic and can be easily scaled up or down as needed.

Security: Security is a top priority when building APIs in Python, as APIs often handle sensitive data and are vulnerable to attacks. Make sure that the tools you choose offer robust security features, such as encryption, authentication, and authorization, to protect your API from malicious actors. Look for tools that have a strong track record of security and are regularly updated to address new threats and vulnerabilities.

well-documented, easy to set up and configure, and have a supportive community of users and developers. Look for tools that have clear and concise documentation, as well as tutorials and examples to help you get started quickly.

Best Tools for Building APIs in Python

Now that we have discussed the importance of choosing the right tools for building APIs in Python and the key considerations to keep in mind, let's take a look at some of the best tools available for building APIs in Python:

Flask: Flask is a lightweight and flexible web framework for building APIs in Python. It is easy to use, highly customizable, and well-suited for building small to medium-sized APIs. Flask offers a simple and intuitive API for defining routes, handling requests, and returning responses, making it a popular choice for developers who want to get up and running quickly.

Django: Django is a full-featured web framework for building APIs in Python. It is designed for building large and complex APIs and offers a wide range of built-in features and tools, such as authentication, authorization, and database integration. Django is well-suited for building robust and scalable APIs that require advanced features and functionality.

FastAPI: FastAPI is a modern web framework for building APIs in Python. It is designed for high performance and productivity, with support for asynchronous programming and automatic validation of request and response data. FastAPI offers a simple and intuitive API for defining routes, handling requests, and returning responses, making it a great choice for developers who want to build fast and efficient APIs.

Chapter 4: Setting Up Your Development Environment

Setting up your development environment for Python is an essential step to start programming efficiently. Here are the basic steps to set up a Python development environment:

1. Install Python

First, you need to install Python on your computer. Go to the official Python website and download the latest version for your operating system (Windows, macOS, Linux).

2. Install a Text Editor or IDE

You will need a text editor or an Integrated Development Environment (IDE) to write and manage your Python code. Some popular options include:

Visual Studio Code (VS Code): A lightweight and powerful text editor with many useful extensions.

PyCharm: A comprehensive and robust IDE, ideal for larger projects.
Jupyter Notebook: Excellent for data analysis and data science.

3. Package Management with pip

pip is the official package manager for Python and is used to install additional libraries and packages. To install a package, you can use the command:

bash

pip install package_name

4. Creating Virtual Environments

Virtual environments allow you to isolate the dependencies of one project from those of another project. To create a virtual environment, use the venv module:

Bash

python -m venv environment_name

To activate the virtual environment:

Windows: environment_name\Scripts\activate
macOS/Linux: source environment_name/bin/activate
5. Setting Up VS Code for Python
If you choose to use VS Code, follow these additional steps:

Install the Python extension for VS Code, available in the Marketplace.

Configure the appropriate Python interpreter for your virtual environment in VS Code. This can be done by clicking the gear icon (settings) at the bottom bar and selecting "Python: Select Interpreter".

5. Verifying the Installation

Check if everything is installed correctly by opening a terminal (command prompt or shell) and running the following commands:

Bash

```
python --version
pip --version
```
You should see the installed versions of Python and pip.

6. Test Your Environment

Create a simple Python file to test if the environment is working correctly. Open your editor or IDE and write:

python

```
print("Hello, World!")
```
Save the file with a .py extension (e.g., hello.py) and run it from the terminal:

bash

```
python hello.py
```
You should see the output Hello, World!.

Additional Resources

Python Documentation: docs.python.org

Installing Python and Required Libraries

Python is a popular programming language that is widely used for various purposes such as web development, data analysis, machine learning, and automation. In order to start using Python, you need to install it on your system along with some required libraries. In this article, we will guide you through the process of installing Python and the necessary libraries.

Installing Python:

Python can be easily installed on Windows, macOS, and

Linux operating systems. Here are the steps to install Python on different operating systems:

Windows:

Visit the official Python website at https://www.python.org/downloads/.
Click on the "Download Python" button to download the latest version of Python for Windows.
Run the downloaded installer and follow the on-screen instructions to install Python on your system.
Make sure to check the box that says "Add Python to PATH" during the installation process to make Python accessible from the command prompt.
Once the installation is complete, you can open the command prompt and type "python" to verify that Python has been installed successfully.

macOS:

Open a web browser and go to the official Python website at https://www.python.org/downloads/.
Click on the "Download Python" button to download the latest version of Python for macOS.
Double-click on the downloaded installer file to start the installation process.
Follow the on-screen instructions to install Python on your macOS system.
Once the installation is complete, you can open the terminal and type "python" to verify that Python has been installed successfully.

Linux:

Open a terminal window and type the following command to install Python on your Linux system:
```
```

sudo apt-get install python3
```
```

Enter your password when prompted and press Enter to confirm the installation.
Once the installation is complete, you can type "python3" in the terminal to verify that Python has been installed successfully.

Required Libraries:

Python comes with a standard library that includes a wide range of modules and packages for various tasks. However, there are also many third-party libraries that you may need to install for specific projects. Here are some of the most commonly used libraries in Python:

NumPy: NumPy is a powerful library for numerical computing in Python. It provides support for large, multi-dimensional arrays and matrices, along with a collection of mathematical functions to operate on these arrays.

To install NumPy, you can use the following command:
```
```

pip install numpy
```
```

Pandas: Pandas is a data manipulation and analysis library for Python. It provides data structures like DataFrames and

Series, along with functions for data cleaning, merging, and reshaping.

To install Pandas, you can use the following command:
```
```

```
pip install pandas
```
```
```

Matplotlib: Matplotlib is a plotting library for Python that allows you to create a wide variety of plots and charts. It is widely used for visualizing data in scientific and engineering applications.

To install Matplotlib, you can use the following command:
```
```

```
pip install matplotlib
```
```
```

Scikit-learn: Scikit-learn is a machine learning library for Python that provides tools for data mining and data analysis. It includes various algorithms for classification, regression, clustering, and dimensionality reduction.

To install Scikit-learn, you can use the following command:
```
```

```
pip install scikit-learn
```
```
```

TensorFlow: TensorFlow is an open-source machine learning library developed by Google. It provides tools for building and training neural networks, along with support for distributed computing and deployment on various platforms.

To install TensorFlow, you can use the following command:
```
```
pip install tensorflow
```
```

Flask: Flask is a lightweight web framework for Python that allows you to build web applications quickly and easily. It provides support for routing, templating, and handling HTTP requests.

To install Flask, you can use the following command:
```
```
pip install Flask

```
```

These are just a few examples of the many libraries available in Python. Depending on your project requirements, you may need to install additional libraries to support specific tasks.

In conclusion, installing Python and the required libraries is a straightforward process that can be done in a few simple steps. By following the instructions provided in this article, you can set up your Python environment and start working on your projects with ease. Python's versatility and extensive library support make it a popular choice among developers for a wide range of applications.

Setting Up a Version Control System in APIs

Setting up a version control system for APIs in any programming language is a crucial step in ensuring the stability, scalability, and maintainability of your API projects. Version control systems allow developers to keep track of changes made to their code, collaborate with team members, and roll back to previous versions if needed. In this article, we will discuss the importance of version control systems for APIs and provide a step-by-step guide on how to set up a version control system in your preferred programming language.

Why Use Version Control Systems for APIs?

Version control systems are essential for APIs for several reasons:

Collaboration: Version control systems allow developers to work together on the same codebase without interfering with each other's work. Team members can easily track changes made by others, merge their changes, and resolve conflicts.

History Tracking: Version control systems keep a record of every change made to the codebase, including who made the change, when it was made, and why it was made. This history tracking is crucial for debugging issues, understanding the evolution of the codebase, and auditing changes.

Rollback: Version control systems allow developers to roll back to previous versions of the codebase if a new change introduces bugs or breaks existing functionality. This rollback feature is essential for maintaining the stability and reliability of APIs.

Branching and Merging: Version control systems support branching and merging, which allow developers to work on new features or bug fixes in isolation without affecting the main codebase. Once the changes are tested and approved, they can be merged back into the main codebase.

Code Review: Version control systems facilitate code reviews by providing a platform for team members to review each other's code, suggest improvements, and ensure code quality and consistency.

Setting Up a Version Control System in Your Preferred Language

Setting up a version control system for APIs in your preferred programming language is a straightforward process that involves the following steps:

Step 1: Choose a Version Control System

The first step in setting up a version control system for APIs is to choose a version control system that meets your requirements. The most popular version control systems used in the industry are Git, Mercurial, and Subversion. Git is the most widely used version control system due to its speed, flexibility, and robust branching and merging capabilities.

Step 2: Install the Version Control System

Once you have chosen a version control system, the next step is to install it on your development machine. Most version control systems provide installation instructions on their official websites. For example, to install Git, you can download and install the Git client from the official Git website.Step 3: Initialize a New Repository
After installing the version control system, you need to initialize a new repository for your API project. To do this, navigate to the root directory of your project in the command line or terminal and run the following command:

```
` ` `

git init
` ` `
```

This command creates a new Git repository in the current directory and initializes it with the necessaryconfiguration files.

Step 4: Add Your API Code to the Repository

Once you have initialized a new repository, you need to add your API code to the repository. To do this, run the following command:

```
` ` `

git add .
` ` `
```

This command adds all the files in the current directory to the staging area, preparing them for the initialcommit.

Step 5: Commit Your Changes

After adding your API code to the repository, you need to commit your changes to create a new snapshot of the codebase. To do this, run the following command:

```
```

git commit -m "Initial commit"
```
```

This command commits the staged changes to the repository with a descriptive message that explains the purpose of the commit.

Step 6: Create a Remote Repository

To collaborate with team members and back up your codebase, you need to create a remote repository on a hosting service like GitHub, GitLab, or Bitbucket. Once you have created a remote repository, you need to linkit to your local repository by running the following command:

```
```

git remote add origin

```
```

This command adds a remote repository with the specified URL as the origin for your local repository.Step 7: Push

Your Changes to the Remote Repository
After linking your local repository to a remote repository,
you need to push your changes to the remote repository to
make them accessible to team members. To do this, run
the following command:

```
`‎`‎`
git push -u origin master
`‎`‎`
```

This command pushes the committed changes in your
local repository to the remote repository on the master
branch.

Step 8: Create Branches for New Features or Bug Fixes

To work on new features or bug fixes in isolation, you need
to create branches in your repository. To create a new
branch, run the following command:

```
`‎`‎`
git checkout -b
`‎`‎`
```

Chapter 5: API Design Best Practices

In this chapter, we will discuss some of the best practices for designing APIs that are easy to use, maintain, and scale. API design is a critical aspect of building software applications, as it defines how different components of the system interact with each other. By following these best practices, you can ensure that your APIs are well-designed and provide a great experience for developers who use them.

Use RESTful principles: REST (Representational State Transfer) is a popular architectural style for designing APIs. It emphasizes using standard HTTP methods (GET, POST, PUT, DELETE) to perform operations on resources. By following RESTful principles, you can make your APIs more intuitive and easier to understand for developers.

Keep endpoints simple and consistent: When designing APIs, it's important to keep endpoints simple and consistent. Use clear and descriptive names for endpoints that indicate what they do. Avoid using cryptic abbreviations or acronyms that may confuse developers. Additionally, make sure that similar endpoints follow the same naming conventions and structure for a consistent user experience.

Use versioning: As your API evolves over time, it's important to provide versioning to ensure backward compatibility. By versioning your APIs, you can make changes to the API without breaking existing client applications. Use version numbers in the URL (e.g., /v1/resource) or headers to indicate which version of the API the client is using.

Provide clear documentation: Good documentation is essential for any API. Make sure to provide detailed documentation that explains how to use each endpoint, what parameters are required, and what responses to expect. Include examples and code snippets to help developers understand how to interact with your API. Consider using tools like Swagger or OpenAPI to generate interactive documentation for your API.

Validate input and handle errors gracefully: When designing APIs, it's important to validate input data to prevent errors and security vulnerabilities. Use input validation techniques such as data type checking, length validation, and format validation to ensure that the data provided by the client is valid. Additionally, handle errors gracefully by providing meaningful error messages and status codes to help developers troubleshoot issues.

Implement rate limiting and authentication: To protect your API from abuse and unauthorized access, implement rate limiting and authentication mechanisms. Rate limiting restricts the number of requests that a client can make to the API within a certain time frame, preventing denial-of-service attacks. Authentication ensures that only authorized users can access the API by requiring API keys, tokens, or other credentials.

Use HATEOAS: HATEOAS (Hypermedia as the Engine of Application State) is a principle that allows APIs to provide links to related resources in the response. By including hypermedia links in your API responses, you can make it easier for developers to navigate and discover other endpoints in the API. This can improve the usability and flexibility of your API.

Monitor and analyze API usage: To ensure the performance and reliability of your API, monitor and analyze its usage regularly. Use tools like API analytics platforms to track metrics such as response times, error rates, and usage patterns. By monitoring API usage, you can identify bottlenecks, optimize performance, and make informed decisions about scaling your API.

Designing APIs that are easy to use, maintain, and scale requires careful planning and attention to detail. By following these best practices, you can create APIs that provide a great experience for developers and help drive the success of your software applications. Remember to keep endpoints simple and consistent, provide clear documentation, validate input, implement rate limiting and authentication, use HATEOAS, and monitor API usage to ensure the success of your API design.

Resource Modeling with python in APIs

Resource modeling is an essential aspect of designing and implementing APIs in any programming language, including Python. In this article, we will explore the concept of resource modeling with Python in APIs and discuss how to effectively implement it in your projects.

What is Resource Modeling?

Resource modeling is the process of representing and defining the data and functionality of resources in an API. A resource is any data entity that can be accessed and manipulated through the API, such as a user, product, or order. Resource modeling involves defining the structure and behavior of these resources, including their attributes, relationships, and actions.

In API design, resources are typically represented using data models, which are classes or data structures that define the properties and methods of a resource. These data models serve as blueprints for creating, updating, and querying resources in the API. By modeling resources effectively, developers can ensure that the API is well-structured, maintainable, and easy to use.

Resource Modeling with Python in APIs

Python is a popular programming language for building APIs due to its simplicity, readability, and versatility. When modeling resources in Python APIs, developers can leverage the language's object-oriented features to define data models that represent the resources in the API. In Python, data models are typically implemented as classes using the `class` keyword.

To illustrate resource modeling with Python in APIs, let's consider an example of a simple e-commerce API that manages products. In this API, we have a `Product` resource that represents a product in the e-commerce store. To model the `Product` resource, we can create a Python class called `Product` with attributes such as `id`, `name`, `price`, and `quantity`.

```python
```python class Product:
def__init__(self, id, name, price, quantity):
self.id = id self.name = nameself.price = price
self.quantity = quantity
```
```

In this example, the `Product` class defines a data model for the `Product` resource with four attributes: `id`, `name`, `price`, and `quantity`. The `__init__` method is a special method in Python that is called when a new instance of the class is created. It initializes the attributes of the `Product` object with the values passed as arguments.

Once we have defined the data model for the `Product` resource, we can use instances of the `Product` class to represent individual products in the API. For example, we can create a list of `Product` objects to store and manipulate multiple products in the e-commerce store.

```python
products = [
Product(1, 'iPhone', 999.99, 10),
Product(2, 'MacBook', 1499.99, 5),
Product(3, 'iPad', 499.99, 20)
]
```

In this code snippet, we create a list of `Product` objects representing three products in the e-commerce store: an iPhone, a MacBook, and an iPad. Each `Product` object contains the attributes `id`, `name`, `price`, and `quantity`, which can be accessed and modified as needed.

In addition to defining data models for resources, resource modeling in Python APIs also involves defining relationships between resources. For example, in our e-commerce API, we may have a `User` resource that represents a user who can purchase products from the store. To model the relationship between users and products, we can introduce a `User` class with a `purchases` attribute that stores the products purchased by the user.

```python
class User:
def __init__(self, id, name):
self.id = id
self.name = name
self.purchases = []

def purchase_product(self, product):
self.purchases.append(product)
```

In this example, the `User` class defines a data model for

the `User` resource with attributes `id`, `name`, and `purchases`. The `purchases` attribute is a list that stores the products purchased by the user. The `purchase_product` method allows a user to purchase a product and add it to their list of purchases.

By modeling resources and relationships in this way, developers can create a well-structured and intuitive API that allows users to interact with resources in a meaningful and efficient manner. Resource modeling with Python in APIs enables developers to define the structure and behavior of resources, manage data effectively, and ensure consistency and coherence in the API design.

Implementing Resource Modeling in Python APIs

To implement resource modeling in Python APIs, developers can use frameworks and libraries that provide tools and utilities for defining data models, managing resources, and handling API requests and responses. One popular framework for building APIs in Python is Django, which includes a powerful Object-Relational Mapping (ORM) system that simplifies the process of modeling resources and interacting with databases.

URL Structuring in APIs

When it comes to designing APIs, one of the key considerations is how to structure the URLs that will be used to access the various resources and endpoints provided by the API. URL structuring is an important aspect of API design as it helps to make the API more user-friendly, intuitive, and easy to use. In this article, we will discuss the importance of URL structuring in APIs and provide some best practices for designing effective URL structures.

Why is URL structuring important in APIs?

URL structuring plays a crucial role in the usability and effectiveness of an API. A well-structured URL can make it easier for developers to understand how to interact with the API and access the resources they need. It can also make the API more intuitive for users, helping them to navigate the various endpoints and resources more easily.

In addition, a well-structured URL can also improve the performance of the API. By organizing resources and endpoints in a logical and efficient manner, developers can minimize the number of requests needed to access the data they require, reducing latency and improving overall performance.

Best practices for URL structuring in APIs

When it comes to designing URL structures for APIs,

there are several best practices that developers should keep in mind. These practices can help to ensure that the API is easy to use, intuitive, and efficient. Some of the key best practices for URL structuring in APIs include:

Use meaningful and descriptive URLs: URLs should be descriptive and easy to understand. They should clearly indicate the purpose of the resource or endpoint being accessed, making it easier for developers to navigate the API. For example, a URL like "/users" is more intuitive and descriptive than a generic URL like"/data".

Use consistent naming conventions: Consistency is key when it comes to URL structuring. Developers should use consistent naming conventions for resources and endpoints throughout the API to make it easier to understand and navigate. For example, all user-related endpoints should follow a similar naming convention, such as "/users/{id}" for accessing a specific user.

Use hierarchical structures: Hierarchical URL structures can help to organize resources and endpoints in a logical and intuitive manner. By grouping related resources together in a hierarchical structure, developers can make it easier to navigate the API and access the data they need. For example, a URL like "/users/{id}/posts"can be used to access the posts made by a specific user.

Use query parameters for filtering and sorting: Query parameters can be used to filter and sort data returned by an API endpoint. By using query parameters, developers can customize the results returned by an endpoint based on specific criteria, such as date range, category, or sorting order. For example, a URL like "/posts?category=technology&sort=date" can be used to retrieve posts in the technology category sorted by date.

Avoid unnecessary complexity: While it's important to provide a clear and intuitive URL structure, developers should also avoid unnecessary complexity. URLs should be simple and easy to understand, without unnecessary levels of nesting or complexity. This can help to prevent confusion and make the API more user-friendly.

Use versioning in URLs: Versioning is an important aspect of API design, as it allows developers to make changes to the API without breaking existing client applications. By including a version number in the URL, developers can ensure that clients are accessing the correct version of the API and prevent compatibility issues. For example, a URL like "/v1/posts" can be used to access version 1 of the posts endpoint.

Provide documentation: Finally, it's important to provide comprehensive documentation for the API, including information on how to use the various endpoints and resources. Documentation should include details on the URL structure, query parameters, authentication methods, and any other relevant information that developers may need to interact with the API effectively.

In conclusion, URL structuring is a critical aspect of API design that can have a significant impact on the usability and effectiveness of an API. By following best practices for URL structuring, developers can create APIs that are easy to use, intuitive, and efficient, providing a better experience for both developers and end-users.

Chapter 6: Versioning Your API

In the world of software development, versioning is a crucial aspect of maintaining and evolving an API. Versioning allows developers to make changes to an API without breaking existing client applications that rely on it. By providing different versions of an API, developers can ensure that clients have access to the functionality they need while also allowing for updates and improvements to be made.

In this chapter, we will explore the importance of versioning your API and discuss best practices for managing and implementing versioning in your own projects.

Why Versioning is Important

Versioning your API is important for several reasons. First and foremost, versioning allows you to make changes to your API without breaking existing client applications. If you were to make a breaking change to your API without versioning, all client applications that rely on the API would be affected, potentially causing widespread issues and downtime.

Versioning also allows you to introduce new features and improvements to your API while still supporting older versions for clients that may not be able to immediately upgrade. This can help ensure a smooth transition for clients as they adopt new versions of your API.

Additionally, versioning can help with documentation and communication. By clearly indicating which version of the API a client is using, developers can easily reference the appropriate documentation and understand the capabilities and limitations of the API.

Best Practices for Versioning Your API

When it comes to versioning your API, there are several best practices to keep in mind. These practices can help ensure that your API is easy to use, maintain, and evolve over time.

Use Semantic Versioning: Semantic versioning is a widely adopted versioning scheme that uses a three-part version number (e.g., 1.2.3) to indicate the significance of changes. By following semantic versioning, you can clearly communicate the impact of each update to your API (major, minor, or patch) and help clients understand how to manage upgrades.

Implement Versioning in the URL: One common approach to versioning is to include the version number in the URL of the API endpoint. For example, you might have endpoints like /api/v1/resource and /api/v2/resource to indicate different versions of the API. This approach is straightforward and easy to understand for both developers and clients.

Support Multiple Versions: It's important to support multiple versions of your API to accommodate clients that may be using different versions. This can involve maintaining older versions of the API for a period of time, providing documentation for each version, and clearly communicating when older versions will be deprecated.

Use Headers for Versioning: Another approach to versioning is to use headers in API requests to specify the desired version. This can be useful for clients that may not be able to easily update the URL they are using to access the API. By including version information in headers, you can provide flexibility and compatibility for a wider range of clients.

Document Changes and Deprecations: As you make updates to your API and introduce new versions, it's important to document these changes and communicate them to clients. This can include release notes, changelogs, and deprecation notices to help clients understand how their applications may be affected and what actions they need to take.

Versioning your API is a critical aspect of API design and development. By following best practices for versioning, you can ensure that your API is flexible, maintainable, and easy to use for clients. Whether you choose to include version numbers in URLs, headers, or elsewhere, the key is to provide clear and consistent versioning that helps clients understand how to interact with your API and manage updates effectively. By implementing versioning in your projects, you can build a more robust and reliable API that can evolve and grow over time.

Authentication and Authorization in APIs

Authentication and authorization are two crucial aspects of securing APIs and ensuring that only authorized users can access the resources they need. In this article, we will discuss the importance of authentication and authorization in APIs and how they work together to protect sensitive data and prevent unauthorized access.

Authentication is the process of verifying the identity of a user or application attempting to access an API. This is typically done by requiring users to provide credentials, such as a username and password, a token, or a certificate. Once the credentials are provided, the API can verify the user's identity by comparing the credentials against a database of known users. If the credentials match, the user is authenticated and granted access to the API.

There are several common methods of authentication used in APIs, including basic authentication, OAuth, and JSON Web Tokens (JWT). Basic authentication involves sending a username and password in the HTTP headers of a request, which is then verified by the API server. OAuth is an open standard for token-based authentication, which allows users to grant third-party applications access to their resources without sharing their credentials.
JWT is a compact and self-contained way of transmitting information between parties as a JSON object, which can be used to authenticate and authorize users in APIs.

Authorization, on the other hand, is the process of

determining what actions a user is allowed to perform once they have been authenticated. This involves defining roles and permissions for users, such as read-only access, write access, or administrative privileges. Authorization is typically implemented using access control lists (ACLs) or role-based access control (RBAC), which specify which resources a user can access and what actions they can perform on those resources.

In APIs, authentication and authorization work together to ensure that only authenticated users with the appropriate permissions can access the resources they need. For example, a user may be authenticated using their username and password, but they may only be authorized to read data from a particular endpoint, not write to it. By implementing both authentication and authorization, APIs can protect sensitive data and prevent unauthorized access.

There are several best practices for implementing authentication and authorization in APIs. One common practice is to use HTTPS to encrypt communication between the client and server, which helps prevent eavesdropping and man-in-the-middle attacks. Another best practice is to use strong authentication methods, such as OAuth or JWT, to verify the identity of users and prevent unauthorized access.

It is also important to properly manage and secure user credentials to prevent data breaches. This includes storing passwords securely using techniques like hashing and salting, and implementing multi-factor authentication to add an extra layer of security. Additionally, APIs should enforce strict access control policies to ensure that users can only access the resources they are authorized to access.

Authentication and authorization are essential components of securing APIs and protecting sensitive data. By implementing strong authentication methods, enforcing strict access control policies, and following best practices for managing user credentials, APIs can prevent unauthorized access and ensure that only authenticated users with the appropriate permissions can access the resources they need.

Securing Endpoints in APIs

Securing endpoints in APIs is a crucial aspect of ensuring the safety and integrity of data being transmitted between different systems. With the increasing reliance on APIs for connecting various applications and services, it has become more important than ever to implement robust security measures to protect against potential threats and attacks.

One of the key challenges in securing endpoints in APIs is the sheer volume and complexity of data being transmitted. APIs often handle sensitive information such as personal data, financial records, and business-critical information, making them a prime target for cybercriminals looking to exploit vulnerabilities in the system.

To address these challenges, organizations must implement a multi-layered approach to securing endpoints in APIs. This includes using encryption to protect data in transit, implementing authentication mechanisms to verify the identity of users and devices, and regularly monitoring and auditing API traffic to detect and respond to any suspicious activity.

Encryption is a fundamental security measure that helps protect data from being intercepted and accessed by unauthorized parties. By encrypting data before it is transmitted over the network, organizations can ensure that even if the data is intercepted, it will be unreadable without the decryption key.

Authentication is another critical aspect of securing endpoints in APIs. By requiring users and devices to authenticate themselves before accessing the API, organizations can verify the identity of the parties involved and ensure that only authorized users are able to access sensitive information.

There are several authentication mechanisms that organizations can use to secure endpoints in APIs, including API keys, OAuth tokens, and digital certificates. Each of these mechanisms has its own strengths and weaknesses, so organizations should carefully consider their specific requirements and choose the most appropriate option for their needs.

In addition to encryption and authentication, organizations must also implement monitoring and auditing mechanisms to detect and respond to any potential security incidents. By monitoring API traffic in real-time and analyzing logs and audit trails, organizations can quickly identify any suspicious activity and take appropriate action to mitigate the threat.

Regular security assessments and penetration testing are also essential to ensuring the security of endpoints in APIs. By regularly testing the security of their APIs and identifying any vulnerabilities or weaknesses, organizations can proactively address potential security risks before they are exploited by malicious actors.

It is also important for organizations to stay up-to-date

with the latest security best practices and standards for securing endpoints in APIs. By following industry guidelines and implementing security controls recommended by experts, organizations can reduce the risk of security breaches and protect their data from unauthorized access.

In conclusion, securing endpoints in APIs is a complex and challenging task that requires a multi-layered approach to ensure the safety and integrity of data being transmitted between different systems.

Chapter 7: Security in API Design

In today's digital world, APIs (Application Programming Interfaces) have become an essential component of software development. APIs allow different software systems to communicate with each other, enabling seamless integration and data exchange. However, with the increased use of APIs, security concerns have also become more prominent. In this chapter, we will discuss the importance of security in API design and provide guidelines for ensuring the security of your APIs.

Security is a critical aspect of API design because APIs are often targeted by malicious actors looking to exploit vulnerabilities for financial gain or to disrupt services. Therefore, it is essential to implement robust security measures to protect sensitive data and prevent unauthorized access. In this chapter, we will explore various security considerations that should be taken into account when designing APIs.

Authentication and Authorization

One of the fundamental security measures in API design is authentication and authorization. Authentication ensures that the user or system accessing the API is who they claim to be, while authorization determines what actions the authenticated user is allowed to perform. Implementing strong authentication mechanisms, such as OAuth or API keys, can help prevent unauthorized access to your API.

Additionally, role-based access control can be used to restrict access to certain API endpoints based on the user's role or permissions. By implementing granular access controls, you can ensure that only authorized users can access sensitive data or perform specific actions.

Data Encryption

Another important aspect of API security is data encryption. Encrypting sensitive data transmitted between the client and the API can help prevent eavesdropping and data breaches. Using HTTPS with SSL/TLS encryption is recommended to ensure secure communication between the client and the API server.

Furthermore, encrypting data at rest can help protect sensitive information stored on the server. By implementing encryption algorithms such as AES or RSA, you can ensure that data is securely stored and only accessible to authorized users.

Input Validation

Input validation is a crucial security measure that helps prevent common vulnerabilities such as SQL injection and cross-site scripting (XSS) attacks. By validating and sanitizing user input before processing it, you can mitigate the risk of malicious code injection and data manipulation.

Implementing input validation mechanisms, such as whitelisting or blacklisting input parameters, can help ensurethat only valid and safe data is accepted by the API. Additionally, using parameterized queries when interactingwith databases can help prevent SQL injection attacks by separating data from SQL commands.

Rate Limiting and Throttling

Rate limiting and throttling are essential security measures that help prevent abuse and protect the API server from overload. By setting limits on the number of requests that can be made within a specific time frame, youcan prevent malicious actors from launching denial-of-service (DoS) attacks or overwhelming the server with excessive traffic.

Implementing rate limiting and throttling mechanisms can help ensure the availability and performance of your API by controlling the rate of incoming requests. By monitoring and analyzing API traffic, you can identify abnormal patterns and take proactive measures to mitigate potential threats.

Monitoring and Logging

Monitoring and logging are essential components of API security that help detect and respond to securityincidents in real-time. By monitoring API traffic, server performance, and user activities, you can identify suspicious behavior and potential security threats.

Implementing logging mechanisms can help track and record API requests, responses, and errors for auditing and troubleshooting purposes. By analyzing log data, you can identify security incidents, track user activities, and investigate potential vulnerabilities.

Conclusion

In conclusion, security is a critical aspect of API design that should not be overlooked. By implementing robust security measures, such as authentication and authorization, data encryption, input validation, rate limiting, andmonitoring, you can protect your APIs from security threats and ensure the confidentiality, integrity, and availability of your data.

In this chapter, we have discussed various security considerations that should be taken into account when designing APIs. By following best practices and guidelines for API security, you can build secure and reliableAPIs that meet the needs of your users and protect sensitive information from unauthorized access.

Remember, security is an ongoing process, and it is essential to regularly update and review your security measures to adapt to new threats and vulnerabilities. By staying informed about the latest security trends and technologies, you can enhance the security of your APIs and maintain the trust of your users.

Common Vulnerabilities and Mitigation in APIs

Application Programming Interfaces (APIs) have become an essential component of modern software development. They allow different software systems to communicate with each other, enabling the exchange of data and services. However, like any other software component, APIs are vulnerable to security threats. In this article, we will discuss some common vulnerabilities in APIs and how to mitigate them.

Injection Attacks
Injection attacks occur when an attacker sends malicious input to an API endpoint, causing the API to execute unintended commands. The most common type of injection attack is SQL injection, where an attacker sends SQL queries as input to the API, potentially giving them access to sensitive data or the ability to manipulate the database.

To mitigate injection attacks, developers should use parameterized queries and input validation to sanitize user input before processing it. Additionally, using stored procedures and prepared statements can help prevent SQL injection attacks.

Broken Authentication
Authentication is a critical component of API security, as it ensures that only authorized users can access the API. Broken authentication vulnerabilities occur when developers fail to properly implement authentication

mechanisms, allowing attackers to bypass authentication and gain unauthorized access to the API.

To mitigate broken authentication vulnerabilities, developers should use strong authentication methods such as OAuth or JWT tokens. Additionally, implementing multi-factor authentication and regularly updating passwords can help prevent unauthorized access to the API.

Cross-Site Scripting (XSS)
Cross-Site Scripting (XSS) attacks occur when an attacker injects malicious scripts into a web application, which are then executed by unsuspecting users. In the context of APIs, XSS attacks can occur when an API endpoint returns user-generated content without proper sanitization, allowing attackers to execute malicious scripts in the context of the user's browser.

To mitigate XSS vulnerabilities, developers should sanitize user input and output to prevent the execution of malicious scripts. Using Content Security Policy (CSP) headers can also help prevent XSS attacks by restricting the types of scripts that can be executed on a web page.

Insecure Direct Object References (IDOR)
Insecure Direct Object References (IDOR) vulnerabilities occur when an attacker can access or manipulate objects in an API by directly referencing them in the request. This can happen when developers fail to properly enforce access controls or use predictable object references, allowing attackers to access sensitive data or perform unauthorized actions.

To mitigate IDOR vulnerabilities, developers should implement proper access controls and enforce authorization checks at each API endpoint. Additionally, using random or non-sequential object references can help prevent attackers from guessing valid object references.

Insecure Deserialization

Insecure deserialization vulnerabilities occur when an attacker can manipulate serialized data sent to an API in order to execute arbitrary code or perform unauthorized actions. This can lead to remote code execution or other security exploits.

To mitigate insecure deserialization vulnerabilities, developers should validate and sanitize serialized data before deserializing it. Additionally, using libraries or frameworks that provide secure deserialization mechanisms can help prevent attackers from exploiting this vulnerability.

Security Misconfigurations
Security misconfigurations occur when developers fail to properly configure security settings in an API, leaving it vulnerable to attacks. This can include using default passwords, exposing sensitive information in error messages, or failing to update software components with known security vulnerabilities.

To mitigate security misconfigurations, developers should follow security best practices such as limiting access to sensitive data, regularly updating software components, and using strong encryption algorithms. Additionally, conducting regular security audits and penetration testing can help identify and address security misconfigurations in an API.

Lack of Rate Limiting

Lack of rate limiting vulnerabilities occur when an API endpoint does not enforce limits on the number of requests that can be made within a certain time period. This can lead to denial of service attacks or brute force attacks, where an attacker sends a large number of requests in a short amount of time in order to overwhelm theAPI.

To mitigate lack of rate limiting vulnerabilities, developers should implement rate limiting mechanisms at eachAPI endpoint to prevent abuse. This can include setting limits on the number of requests per user, IP address, orAPI key, as well as implementing strategies to detect and block malicious traffic.

Insufficient Logging and Monitoring

Insufficient logging and monitoring vulnerabilities occur when developers fail to properly log and monitor API activity, making it difficult to detect and respond to security incidents. This can allow attackers to carry out attacks without being detected, potentially causing significant damage to the API and its users.

To mitigate insufficient logging and monitoring vulnerabilities, developers should implement comprehensive logging and monitoring mechanisms that capture and analyze API activity in real-time. This can include logginguser authentication events, API requests and responses, and error messages, as well as setting up alerts for suspicious or anomalous activity.

APIs are a critical component of modern software development, but they are also vulnerable to a variety of security threats.

Importance of API Documentation

API documentation plays a crucial role in the development and implementation of software applications. It provides developers with the information they need to effectively integrate and use an API within their own projects. In this article, we will discuss the importance of API documentation in software development and why it is essential for developers to have access to clear and comprehensive documentation when working with APIs.

First and foremost, API documentation serves as a guide for developers who are looking to integrate an API into their applications. It provides detailed information on how the API works, what endpoints are available, and how to make requests to the API. Without proper documentation, developers would be left to figure out how to use the API on their own, which can be a time-consuming and frustrating process.

Additionally, API documentation helps to ensure consistency and accuracy in the implementation of the API. By providing clear and detailed instructions on how to use the API, developers can avoid making mistakes or using the API in unintended ways. This can help to prevent errors and bugs in the software, ultimately leading to a more reliable and stable application.

Furthermore, API documentation can also serve as a reference for developers who are looking to troubleshoot issues or make improvements to their code. By providing detailed information on the API's functionality and usage, developers can quickly identify and address any problems that may arise during the development process. This can help to streamline the development process and ensure that the software is of the highest quality.

In addition to providing information on how to use the API, documentation can also include examples and code snippets to help developers better understand how the API works. This can be especially helpful for developers who are new to using the API or who are looking to implement specific features within their applications. By providing real-world examples and practical guidance, documentation can help developers to quickly get up to speed and start using the API effectively.

Another important aspect of API documentation is that it can help to improve collaboration and communication between developers. By providing a clear and comprehensive guide to the API, developers can easily share information and work together on integrating the API into their projects. This can help to foster a more collaborative and productive development environment, ultimately leading to better results for the software project.

Moreover, API documentation can also serve as a marketing tool for the API provider. By providing clear and detailed documentation, API providers can attract more developers to use their API and encourage them to build innovative applications with it. Good documentation can help to showcase the capabilities and benefits of the

API, leading to increased adoption and usage among developers.

In conclusion, API documentation is an essential component of software development that provides developers with the information they need to effectively integrate and use APIs within their applications. By providing clear and comprehensive documentation, developers can avoid errors, troubleshoot issues, and collaborate more effectively on software projects. API documentation also serves as a marketing tool for API providers, helping to attract more developers and promote the use of their APIs. Overall, API documentation plays a crucial role in the success of software projects and should be prioritized by developers and API providers alike.

Chapter 8: Documentation and Testing

In the world of software development, documentation and testing are two crucial components that ensure the success and quality of a project. In this chapter, we will explore the importance of documentation and testing, aswell as best practices for implementing them effectively.

Documentation is the process of creating and maintaining written materials that provide information about a software project. This includes everything from user manuals and technical specifications to code comments anddesign documents. Documentation plays a key role in ensuring that a project is well-documented, easy to understand, and maintainable.

One of the main benefits of documentation is that it helps developers and other stakeholders understand the purpose and functionality of a software project. By documenting the requirements, design decisions, and implementation details of a project, developers can easily track changes, troubleshoot issues, and collaboratewith team members.

Additionally, documentation serves as a valuable resource for onboarding new team members. When a newdeveloper joins a project, they can quickly get up to speed by referring to the project's documentation. Thissaves time and reduces the risk of misunderstandings or errors.

Another important aspect of documentation is that it helps ensure the long-term maintainability of a project. By documenting the codebase, developers can easily identify and fix bugs, make enhancements, and refactor code without introducing new issues. This is especially important for large and complex projects that require frequent updates and modifications.

In addition to code documentation, it is also important to document the testing process. Testing is the process of evaluating a software project to ensure that it meets the specified requirements and functions correctly. Testing helps identify bugs, performance issues, and other problems that may impact the quality and reliability of a project.

There are several types of testing that can be performed on a software project, including unit testing, integration testing, system testing, and acceptance testing. Each type of testing serves a different purpose and helps ensure that the project is free of defects and meets the specified requirements.

Unit testing involves testing individual components or modules of a project in isolation. This helps identify bugs and errors at the code level and ensures that each component functions correctly. Integration testing involves testing how different components interact with each other and ensures that they work together as expected.

System testing involves testing the entire system as a whole to ensure that it meets the specified requirements and functions correctly. This includes testing the user interface, performance, security, and other aspects of the project. Acceptance testing involves testing the project with end users to ensure that it meets their needs and expectations.

In addition to testing, it is important to document the testing process to ensure that it is thorough, repeatable, and well-documented. This includes documenting the test cases, test results, and any issues or bugs that are identified during testing. By documenting the testing process, developers can easily track the progress of testing, identify areas for improvement, and ensure that the project meets the specified requirements.

Documentation and testing are two essential components of software development that help ensure the success and quality of a project. By documenting the requirements, design decisions, and implementation details of a project, developers can easily understand and maintain the project.

Additionally, by testing the project thoroughly and documenting the testing process, developers can identify and fix bugs, performance issues, and other problems that may impact the quality and reliability of the project. By following best practices for documentation and testing, developers can ensure that their projects are well-documented, easy to understand, and free of defects.

Tools for API Documentation

API documentation plays a crucial role in helping developers understand and integrate with an application programming interface (API). Without proper documentation, developers may struggle to effectively use an API, leading to frustration and inefficiencies in the development process. To address this need, there are a variety of tools available to help developers create comprehensive and user-friendly API documentation. In this article, we will explore some of the top tools for API documentation in the language.

Swagger:
Swagger is one of the most popular tools for API documentation. It allows developers to create interactive and visually appealing documentation for their APIs. Swagger provides a user-friendly interface that makes it easy for developers to explore and test different endpoints. It also supports various programming languages, making it a versatile choice for API documentation.

Swagger also offers a range of features, including the ability to generate code snippets in multiple languages, validate API requests, and automatically generate API documentation from code annotations. This makes it a powerful tool for developers looking to streamline the documentation process and ensure that their APIs are well-documented and easy to use.

Postman:

Postman is another popular tool for API documentation that offers a range of features to help developers create comprehensive documentation for their APIs. Postman allows developers to create collections of API requests, organize them into folders, and share them with team members. It also provides a user-friendly interface that makes it easy to test and debug API requests.

Postman also offers a range of collaboration features, including the ability to share documentation with team members, track changes, and comment on specific requests. This makes it a great choice for teams looking to work together to create and maintain API documentation.

Apiary:
Apiary is a comprehensive API documentation tool that offers a range of features to help developers create and maintain documentation for their APIs. Apiary allows developers to define API endpoints, request and response formats, and authentication requirements using a simple and intuitive interface. It also provides a range of customization options, allowing developers to create documentation that fits their specific needs.

Apiary also offers a range of collaboration features, including the ability to share documentation with team members, track changes, and comment on specific endpoints. This makes it a great choice for teams looking to work together to create and maintain API documentation.

Stoplight:
Stoplight is a powerful API documentation tool that offers

a range of features to help developers create and maintain documentation for their APIs. Stoplight allows developers to define API endpoints, request and response formats, and authentication requirements using a simple and intuitive interface. It also provides a range of customization options, allowing developers to create documentation that fits their specific needs.

Stoplight also offers a range of collaboration features, including the ability to share documentation with team members, track changes, and comment on specific endpoints. This makes it a great choice for teams looking to work together to create and maintain API documentation.

Slate:

Slate is a lightweight API documentation tool that offers a simple and intuitive interface for creating and maintaining documentation for APIs. Slate allows developers to define API endpoints, request and response formats, and authentication requirements using a Markdown-based syntax. It also provides a range of customization options, allowing developers to create documentation that fits their specific needs.

Slate also offers a range of collaboration features, including the ability to share documentation with team members, track changes, and comment on specific endpoints. This makes it a great choice for teams looking to work together to create and maintain API documentation.

There are a variety of tools available to help developers create comprehensive and user-friendly API documentation in the language. Whether you choose Swagger, Postman, Apiary, Stoplight, Slate, or another tool, it is important to invest time and effort into creating high-quality API documentation to ensure that developers can effectively integrate with your API.

By using the right tools and following best practices, you can create documentation that is clear, concise, and easy to use, ultimately leading to a more seamless and efficient development process.

Writing Effective Tests for APIs with python

Writing effective tests for APIs with Python is crucial for ensuring the reliability and stability of your application. APIs (Application Programming Interfaces) are the backbone of modern software development, allowing different systems to communicate with each other. By testing your APIs thoroughly, you can catch bugs early, ensure that your code works as expected, and provide a better user experience for your customers.

In this article, we will discuss the importance of writing tests for APIs, the different types of tests you can write, and how to write effective tests using Python.

Why Write Tests for APIs?

Writing tests for APIs is important for several reasons:

Ensure the correctness of your code: Testing your APIs helps ensure that your code works as expected and produces the correct results. By writing tests, you can catch bugs early in the development process and prevent them from reaching production.

Improve code quality: Writing tests forces you to think about how your code should behave in different scenarios. This can lead to cleaner, more maintainable code that is easier to understand and work with.

Increase confidence in your code: By writing tests for your

APIs, you can have confidence that your code is working correctly and that any changes you make in the future will not break existing functionality.

Facilitate collaboration: Tests serve as a form of documentation for your code, making it easier for other developers to understand how your APIs work and how they should be used.

Types of Tests for APIs

There are several types of tests that you can write for APIs, each serving a different purpose:

Unit tests: Unit tests focus on testing individual components or functions in isolation. These tests are typically fast to run and provide quick feedback on the correctness of your code.

Integration tests: Integration tests verify that different components of your application work together correctly. These tests are useful for testing interactions between different parts of your code and for identifying issues that may arise when components are combined.

End-to-end tests: End-to-end tests simulate real-world user scenarios and test the entire application from start to finish. These tests are slower to run but provide valuable insights into how your application behaves in a production environment.

Performance tests: Performance tests measure the speed and efficiency of your APIs under different loads. These tests help identify bottlenecks and performance issues that may impact the user experience.

Security tests: Security tests check for vulnerabilities in your APIs, such as SQL injection or cross-site scripting attacks. These tests are essential for ensuring that your APIs are secure and protected from malicious actors.

Writing Effective Tests with Python

Python is a popular programming language for writing tests due to its simplicity, readability, and extensive testing libraries. Here are some tips for writing effective tests for APIs with Python:

Use a testing framework: Python has several testing frameworks, such as unittest, pytest, and nose, that make it easy to write and run tests. Choose a framework that best suits your needs and familiarize yourself with its features.

Write clear and descriptive test names: Give your tests descriptive names that clearly indicate what is being tested. This makes it easier to understand the purpose of each test and helps identify issues when tests fail.

Use fixtures: Fixtures are reusable pieces of code that set up the environment for your tests. By using fixtures, you can avoid duplicating code and ensure that your tests run in a consistent and predictable manner.

Mock external dependencies: When testing APIs, you may need to interact with external services or databases. Use mocking libraries, such as unittest.mock or pytest-mock, to simulate these dependencies and isolate your tests from external factors.

Test edge cases: Test your APIs with different input values, boundary conditions, and error scenarios to ensure that your code handles all possible scenarios correctly. This helps identify potential bugs and edge cases that may not be immediately obvious.

Use assertions: Use assertions to verify that your code produces the expected output. Python's built-in assert statement is a powerful tool for writing assertions in your tests and checking that your code behaves as expected.

Run tests automatically: Set up a continuous integration (CI) system, such as Jenkins or Travis CI, to automatically run your tests whenever code changes are made. This ensures that your tests are always up-to-date and provides immediate feedback on the quality of your code.

Monitor test coverage: Use tools like coverage.py to measure the test coverage of your code. Aim for high test coverage to ensure that all parts of your code are tested and that potential bugs are caught early.

Writing effective tests for APIs with Python is essential for ensuring the reliability and stability of your application. By writing tests, you can catch bugs early, improve code quality, increase confidence in your code, and provide a better user experience for your customers.

Chapter 9: Building RESTful APIs with Python

In this chapter, we will explore how to build RESTful APIs using Python. RESTful APIs are a popular way to allow different systems to communicate with each other over the internet. They use HTTP methods such as GET, POST, PUT, DELETE to perform operations on resources. Python is a versatile and powerful programming language that is well-suited for building APIs due to its simplicity and readability.

To build RESTful APIs in Python, we will be using the Flask framework. Flask is a lightweight and easy-to-use web framework that allows you to create web applications and APIs quickly. It provides tools and libraries that make it easy to handle HTTP requests, route URLs, and serialize data to and from JSON.

Setting up Flask is simple. You can install Flask using pip, a package manager for Python. Once Flask is installed, you can create a new Flask application by creating a new Python file and importing the Flask module. You can then define routes and methods to handle different HTTP requests.

To create a RESTful API with Flask, you need to define routes for different resources and HTTP methods. For example, you can define a route for a list of users using the GET method to retrieve all users, and a route for creating a new user using the POST method. You can also define routes for updating and deleting users using thePUT and DELETE methods, respectively.

When defining routes in Flask, you can use route decorators to specify the URL path and the HTTP methods that the route should handle. For example, you can use the @app.route decorator to define a route for the /users URL path and specify that it should handle GET requests.

Flask also provides tools for serializing data to and from JSON. You can use the jsonify function to serialize Python objects to JSON format, and the request.json attribute to parse JSON data from incoming requests. Thismakes it easy to send and receive data in JSON format, which is a common format used in RESTful APIs.

In addition to handling HTTP requests and serializing data, Flask also allows you to define middleware functions to perform additional processing on incoming requests. Middleware functions can be used to authenticate users, validate input data, or perform other tasks before passing the request to the route handler.

Overall, building RESTful APIs with Python and Flask is a straightforward process that allows you to createpowerful and flexible APIs for your applications. By defining routes, handling HTTP requests, and serializingdata to and from JSON, you can create APIs that can be easily consumed by other systems and applications.

In the next chapter, we will explore how to deploy and test

RESTful APIs built with Python and Flask. We will cover topics such as deploying APIs to cloud platforms, writing unit tests for APIs, and monitoring API performance. Stay tuned for more exciting content on building and working with RESTful APIs in Python.

Why Choose Flask?

Flask is a popular and powerful web framework for building web applications in Python. It is known for its simplicity, flexibility, and ease of use, making it a top choice for developers looking to create web applications quickly and efficiently. In this article, we will explore the reasons why Flask is a great choice for building web applications.

One of the main reasons why developers choose Flask is its simplicity. Flask is designed to be easy to learn and use, with a minimalistic approach that allows developers to focus on writing code without getting bogged down in complex frameworks and libraries. The Flask framework is lightweight and unobtrusive, making it easy to getstarted with and customize to fit the needs of your project.

Another reason why developers choose Flask is its flexibility. Flask is a microframework, which means that it provides the basic tools and features needed to build a web application, but allows developers to add additional functionality as needed. This flexibility allows developers to create web applications that are tailored to their specific requirements, without being limited by the constraints of a larger, more rigid framework.

Flask also has a strong community of developers who contribute to the framework and provide support through forums, documentation, and tutorials. This active community ensures that Flask remains up-to-date and well- maintained, with new features and improvements being added regularly. Developers can rely on the Flask community for help and guidance when building web applications, making it a reliable and trusted choice for web development projects.

In addition to its simplicity and flexibility, Flask is also known for its performance. Flask is lightweight and efficient, with a minimal footprint that allows web applications to run quickly and smoothly. This performance is crucial for web applications that need to handle large amounts of traffic and data, ensuring that users have a seamless and responsive experience when using the application.

Flask also has a clear and intuitive API that makes it easy to work with and understand. The Flask API is well-documented and easy to navigate, with clear examples and explanations that help developers get up to speed quickly. This simplicity and clarity make Flask a great choice for developers who are new to web development, as well as experienced developers looking for a straightforward and efficient framework.

Another reason why developers choose Flask is its extensibility. Flask provides a wide range of extensions and plugins that allow developers to add additional functionality to their web applications with ease. These extensions cover a variety of features, such as authentication, database integration, caching, and more, making it easy to enhance the functionality of your web application without having to write code from scratch.

Flask also supports a range of third-party libraries and tools that can be integrated with the framework to add even more functionality to your web application. This extensibility allows developers to leverage existing libraries and tools to build web applications quickly and efficiently, without having to reinvent the wheel. Flask's support for third-party libraries and tools makes it a versatile and powerful choice for web development projectsof all sizes and complexity.

Flask is a great choice for developers looking to build web applications quickly and efficiently. Its simplicity, flexibility, performance, and extensibility make it a top choice for web development projects of all sizes and complexity.

Whether you are a beginner looking to learn web development or an experienced developer looking for a reliable and efficient framework, Flask has something to offer. Give Flask a try and seefor yourself why it is one of the most popular web frameworks for building web applications in Python.

Setting Up a Flask Project with python

Flask is a popular web framework for building web applications using Python. It is lightweight, easy to use, and highly customizable, making it a great choice for developers looking to quickly set up a web project. In this article, we will guide you through the process of setting up a Flask project with Python.

Step 1: Install Flask

The first step in setting up a Flask project is to install Flask. You can do this by using pip, the Python package manager. Open a terminal window and run the following command:

```
```

pip install Flask
```
```

This will download and install Flask and its dependencies on your system.Step 2: Create a Project Directory
Once Flask is installed, you can create a new directory for your project. Navigate to the directory where you want to create your project and run the following command:

```
```

mkdir my_flask_projectcd my_flask_project
```
```

This will create a new directory called my_flask_project

and navigate you into it. Step 3: Create a Virtual Environment

It is a good practice to create a virtual environment for your Flask project to isolate its dependencies from other projects on your system. To create a virtual environment, run the following command:

```
```
python -m venv venv
```
```

This will create a new directory called venv inside your project directory, which will contain all the dependencies for your project.

Step 4: Activate the Virtual Environment

Once the virtual environment is created, you need to activate it. On Windows, you can activate the virtual environment by running the following command:

```
```

```
venv\Scripts\activate
```

On macOS and Linux, you can activate the virtual environment by running the following command:

```
source venv/bin/activate
```

You will know that the virtual environment is activated when you see (venv) in front of your command prompt.
Step 5: Create a Flask Application
Now that you have set up your project directory and virtual environment, you can create a Flask application. Create a new Python file called app.py in your project directory and open it in a text editor. Add the following code to create a simple Flask application:

```python
from flask import Flaskapp = Flask(___name_)
@app.route('/') def hello_world():
return 'Hello, World!'

if___name_== '__main_':
app.run()
```

This code creates a new Flask application with a single route that returns "Hello, World!" when you visit the root URL of the application.

Step 6: Run the Flask Application

To run your Flask application, open a terminal window, activate your virtual environment, and run the following command:

```
python app.py
```

This will start the Flask development server, and you will see output similar to the following:

```
* Running on http://127.0.0.1:5000/ (Press CTRL+C to quit)
```

Open a web browser and navigate to http://127.0.0.1:5000/ to see your Flask application in action. You should see a page that displays "Hello, World!".

Step 7: Install Additional Packages

Flask is a lightweight framework, but you may need to install additional packages to add functionality to your project. You can install additional packages using pip inside your virtual environment. For example, if you want to use Flask-SQLAlchemy to work with a database, you can install it by running the following command:

```
pip install Flask-SQLAlchemy
```

Step 8: Structure Your Project

As your Flask project grows, you may want to organize your code into separate files and directories. A common way to structure a Flask project is to create a directory for your application code, templates, and static files. You can create a structure like the following:

```
my_flask_project/venv/
app.py requirements.txtmy_app/
_____init___.pymodels.py routes.py templates/ static/
```

In this structure, the app.py file contains the main Flask application, the my_app directory contains the application code, models.py contains database models, routes.py contains route definitions, templates/ contains HTML templates, and static/ contains static files like CSS and JavaScript.

Step 9: Use a Configuration File

It is a good practice to store configuration settings in a separate file rather than hardcoding them in your application code. You can create a configuration file called config.py in your project directory and add configuration settings like database URLs, secret keys, and other settings. You can then import these settingsinto your Flask application using the app.config.from_pyfile() method.

Step 10: Use Blueprints

As your Flask project grows, you may want to split your application into smaller modules called blueprints.

Chapter 10: Routing and Request Handling

Routing and request handling are essential components of any web application. In this chapter, we will explore how routing works and how requests are handled in a web application.

Routing is the process of determining which code to execute based on the URL of a request. When a user enters a URL in their browser, the web server needs to know which code to execute to generate the appropriate response. This is where routing comes into play.

In most web applications, routing is handled by a router. The router is responsible for mapping URLs to specific code that will handle the request. This mapping is typically done using a set of rules defined by the developer.

For example, let's say we have a simple web application with two pages: a homepage and a contact page. The router would have rules that map the URL "/home" to the code that generates the homepage and the URL "/contact" to the code that generates the contact page.

When a user enters one of these URLs in their browser, the router will match the URL to the appropriate rule and execute the corresponding code. This code will generate the HTML for the page and send it back to the user's browser.

109

In addition to mapping URLs to specific code, routers can also handle dynamic URLs. Dynamic URLs contain parameters that can change based on user input. For example, a blog website might have URLs like "/post/123" where "123" is the ID of a specific blog post.

The router can extract the parameter from the URL and pass it to the code that handles the request. This allowsthe code to generate a response based on the specific parameter provided by the user.

Request handling is the process of generating a response to a user's request. This response can be in the form of HTML, JSON, or any other type of data that the user's browser can understand.

In most web applications, request handling is done by controllers. Controllers are responsible for executing the code that generates the response to a user's request. They interact with models to retrieve data from a database, process that data, and generate the appropriate response.

For example, let's say a user submits a form on a web page. The controller responsible for handling form submissions will retrieve the data from the form, validate it, and save it to the database. It will then generate a response confirming that the form was submitted successfully.

Controllers can also handle other types of requests, such as AJAX requests or API calls. They can generateresponses in different formats, such as JSON or XML, depending on the needs of the application.

In addition to controllers, middleware is another important component of request handling. Middleware is code that runs before or after the controller code. It can perform tasks such as authentication, logging, or error handling.

Middleware can be used to intercept requests before they reach the controller, allowing developers to perform tasks such as checking if a user is authenticated before allowing them to access certain pages.

Overall, routing and request handling are crucial components of any web application. They determine how requests are processed and responses are generated, allowing developers to create dynamic and interactive web applications. By understanding how routing and request handling work, developers can build efficient and user-friendly web applications that meet the needs of their users.

Creating RESTful Endpoints with python - exemple scripts

Creating RESTful endpoints in Python typically involves using a web framework. One of the most popular frameworks for this purpose is Flask, which is lightweight and easy to use. Below is an example of how to set up a simple RESTful API using Flask.

Step 1: Install Flask
First, you need to install Flask. You can do this using pip:

bash

pip install flask

Step 2: Create a Basic Flask Application

Create a new file, e.g., app.py, and add the following code to set up a basic Flask application:

```python
Copiar código
from flask import Flask, jsonify, request

app = Flask(__name__)

# Sample data to act as our database
items = [
    {"id": 1, "name": "Item One", "description": "This is item one"},
```

```python
    {"id": 2, "name": "Item Two", "description": "This is
item two"}
]

# Home route
@app.route('/')
def home():
    return "Welcome to the Flask RESTful API!"

# Get all items
@app.route('/items', methods=['GET'])
def get_items():
    return jsonify(items)

# Get a single item by id
@app.route('/items/<int:item_id>', methods=['GET'])
def get_item(item_id):
    item = next((item for item in items if item["id"] ==
item_id), None)
    if item is not None:
        return jsonify(item)
    return jsonify({"error": "Item not found"}), 404

# Create a new item
@app.route('/items', methods=['POST'])
def create_item():
    new_item = request.get_json()
    new_item["id"] = items[-1]["id"] + 1 if items else 1
    items.append(new_item)
    return jsonify(new_item), 201

# Update an existing item
@app.route('/items/<int:item_id>', methods=['PUT'])
```

```python
def update_item(item_id):
    item = next((item for item in items if item["id"] ==
item_id), None)
    if item is None:
        return jsonify({"error": "Item not found"}), 404
    updated_data = request.get_json()
    item.update(updated_data)
    return jsonify(item)

# Delete an item
@app.route('/items/<int:item_id>',
methods=['DELETE'])
def delete_item(item_id):
    global items
    items = [item for item in items if item["id"] != item_id]
    return jsonify({"message": "Item deleted"})

if __name__ == '__main__':
    app.run(debug=True)
```

Step 3: Run the Flask Application

To run your Flask application, execute the following command in your terminal:

bash

python app.py

Explanation

Home Route: A simple welcome message.

Get All Items: Returns a list of all items.

Get a Single Item: Returns a single item by its ID.

Create Item: Allows you to create a new item. The new item's data is sent in the request body as JSON.

Update Item: Allows you to update an existing item. The updated data is sent in the request body as JSON.

Delete Item: Deletes an item by its ID.

Testing the API
You can test the API using tools like Postman or curl commands in the terminal. Here are some examples using curl:

Get all items:

```bash
Copiar código
curl http://127.0.0.1:5000/items
```
Get a single item:

```bash
Copiar código
curl http://127.0.0.1:5000/items/1
```
Create a new item:

```bash
Copiar código
curl -X POST -H "Content-Type: application/json" -d '{"name": "Item Three", "description": "This is item three"}' http://127.0.0.1:5000/items
```
Update an item:

bash
Copiar código
```
curl -X PUT -H "Content-Type: application/json" -d
'{"name": "Updated Item", "description": "Updated
description"}' http://127.0.0.1:5000/items/1
```
Delete an item:

bash
Copiar código
```
curl   -X   DELETE   http://127.0.0.1:5000/items/
```

Handling Different HTTP Methods with python - scripts

HTTP methods are an essential part of web development as they allow us to interact with web servers and perform various actions like retrieving data, submitting data, updating data, and deleting data. In this article, we will explore how to handle different HTTP methods with Python by using example scripts in the Flask framework.

Flask is a lightweight web framework for Python that allows you to build web applications quickly and easily. It provides a simple way to handle HTTP requests and responses, making it an ideal choice for building RESTful APIs.

In Flask, you can define routes for different HTTP methods like GET, POST, PUT, and DELETE by using the `@app.route` decorator. This decorator takes the URL pattern as an argument and allows you to specify the HTTP methods that the route should respond to.

Let's start by creating a simple Flask application that handles different HTTP methods:

```python
from flask import Flask, requestapp = Flask(__name_)
@app.route('/data', methods=['GET'])def get_data():
return 'This is a GET request'

@app.route('/data', methods=['POST'])def post_data():
```

```python
    data = request.get_json()
    return f'This is a POST request with data: {data}'

@app.route('/data', methods=['PUT'])def put_data():
    data = request.get_json()
    return f'This is a PUT request with data: {data}'

@app.route('/data',        methods=['DELETE'])     def
delete_data():
    return 'This is a DELETE request'

if____name_== '__main_':
    app.run(debug=True)
```

In this example, we have defined four routes for the
`/data` URL pattern, each handling a different HTTP
method. The `get_data` function responds to GET
requests, the `post_data` function responds to POST
requests, the `put_data` function responds to PUT
requests, and the `delete_data` function responds to
DELETE requests.

To test these routes, you can use a tool like Postman to send requests to the Flask application. For example, you can send a GET request to `http://localhost:5000/data` to see the response from the `get_data` function.

You can also send a POST request with JSON data to `http://localhost:5000/data` to see the response from the `post_data` function. Similarly, you can send PUT and DELETE requests to test the `put_data` and `delete_data` functions.

Handling different HTTP methods in Flask is straightforward, and you can easily extend this example to handle more complex scenarios. For example, you can add authentication and authorization checks, input validation, error handling, and database operations to your routes to build a fully functional RESTful API.

In addition to handling different HTTP methods in Flask, you can also use the `requests` library in Python to send HTTP requests to external web servers. This library provides a simple and intuitive way to interact with web APIs and retrieve data from remote servers.

Let's look at an example script that uses the `requests` library to send GET, POST, PUT, and DELETE requests to a RESTful API:

```python
import requests

# GET request
response = requests.get('https://jsonplaceholder.typicode.com/posts/
```

```
1')print(response.json())

# POST request
data = {'title': 'foo', 'body': 'bar', 'userId': 1}
response                                        =
requests.post('https://jsonplaceholder.typicode.com/post
s', json=data)print(response.json())

# PUT request
data = {'title': 'foo', 'body': 'bar', 'userId': 1}
response                                        =
requests.put('https://jsonplaceholder.typicode.com/posts
/1', json=data)print(response.json())

# DELETE request
response                                        =
requests.delete('https://jsonplaceholder.typicode.com/pos
ts/1')print(response.json())
```

In this example, we are sending GET, POST, PUT, and DELETE requests to the JSONPlaceholder API, which provides a mock RESTful API for testing purposes. We use the `requests.get`, `requests.post`, `requests.put`, and `requests.delete` functions to send the corresponding HTTP requests and retrieve the responses.

By using the `requests` library in Python, you can easily interact with web APIs and perform various actions like retrieving data, submitting data, updating data, and deleting data. This makes it a powerful tool for building webapplications that communicate with external services and APIs.

Handling different HTTP methods with Python is essential for building web applications and APIs that interact with web servers. Whether you are using the Flask framework to create a web application or the `requests` library to send HTTP requests to external APIs, Python provides a simple and intuitive way to work with HTTP methods and perform various actions over the web.

Chapter 11: Building APIs with Flask using python

In this chapter, we will explore how to build APIs using the Flask framework in Python. APIs, or Application Programming Interfaces, are a set of rules and protocols that allow different software applications to communicate with each other. By building APIs with Flask, we can create web services that can be accessed and interacted with by other applications.

Flask is a lightweight and flexible web framework for Python that makes it easy to build web applications and APIs. It provides a simple and easy-to-use interface for creating routes, handling requests, and returning responses. Flask is also highly extensible, allowing developers to add additional functionality through plugins and extensions.

To get started building APIs with Flask, we first need to install the Flask framework. We can do this using the pip package manager by running the following command:

```
pip install Flask
```

Once Flask is installed, we can create a new Python file for our API and import the Flask module:

```python
from flask import Flask
```

Next, we can create a new instance of the Flask class to represent our API:

```python
app = Flask(_name_)
```

We can then define routes for our API using the `@app.route` decorator. Routes are URLs that our API will respond to, and we can define different routes for different endpoints of our API. For example, we can create a route that responds to requests to the `/hello` endpoint:

```python
@app.route('/hello')  def hello():
return 'Hello, World!'
```

In this example, the `hello` function will be called when a GET request is made to the `/hello` endpoint, and it will return the string 'Hello, World!'. We can test this route by running our Flask application and making a GET request to the `/hello` endpoint using a web browser or a tool like cURL.

Flask also allows us to handle different types of requests, such as POST, PUT, and DELETE, by specifying the methods parameter of the `@app.route` decorator. For example, we can create a route that accepts POST requests to the `/add` endpoint:

123

```python
@app.route('/add', methods=['POST'])def add():
# Add logic here return 'Added item'
```

In this example, the `add` function will be called when a POST request is made to the `/add` endpoint, and it will return the string 'Added item'. We can test this route by sending a POST request to the `/add` endpoint with a tool like cURL or Postman.

Flask also allows us to return JSON responses from our API by using the `jsonify` function. JSON (JavaScript Object Notation) is a lightweight data-interchange format that is easy for humans to read and write and easy for machines to parse and generate. For example, we can create a route that returns a JSON response with a list of items:

```python
from flask import jsonify

@app.route('/items')  def items():
items = ['item1', 'item2', 'item3']return jsonify(items)
```

In this example, the `items` function will return a JSON response with a list of items when a GET request is made to the `/items` endpoint. We can test this route by making a GET request to the `/items` endpoint using a web browser or a tool like cURL.

Flask also allows us to handle query parameters in our routes by using the `request` object. The `request` object provides access to the incoming request data, such as form data, query parameters, and files. For example, we can create a route that accepts a query parameter called `name`:

```python
from flask import request

@app.route('/greet') def greet():
name   =   request.args.get('name')   return   'Hello, {}!'.format(name)
```

In this example, the `greet` function will return a personalized greeting when a GET request is made to the `/greet` endpoint with a `name` query parameter. We can test this route by making a GET request to the `/greet` endpoint with a `name` query parameter using a web browser or a tool like cURL.

In conclusion, building APIs with Flask using Python is a powerful and flexible way to create web services that can be accessed and interacted with by other applications. By following the examples and techniques outlined in this chapter, you can create your own APIs with Flask and take advantage of the many features and capabilities that Flask has to offer. Happy coding!

Returning JSON Responses with python - scripts

JSON (JavaScript Object Notation) is a lightweight data interchange format that is easy for humans to read and write and easy for machines to parse and generate. It is commonly used for transmitting data between a server and a web application. In this article, we will discuss how to return JSON responses with Python using scripts examples.

Python is a powerful and versatile programming language that is widely used for web development, data analysis, machine learning, and more. It has built-in support for working with JSON data, making it easy to create and parse JSON objects.

To return JSON responses with Python, we can use the built-in `json` module. This module provides functions for encoding Python objects as JSON strings and decoding JSON strings into Python objects. We can use these functions to convert Python dictionaries, lists, and other data structures into JSON format and send them as responses to HTTP requests.

Here is an example of a simple Python script that returns a JSON response:

```python
python import json
from flask import Flaskapp = Flask(___name_)
@app.route('/')def index():
data    =    {'message':    'Hello,    World!'}    return
```

```
json.dumps(data)

if____name_== '__main_':
app.run()
```

In this script, we first import the `json` module and the `Flask` class from the `flask` module. We then create a new `Flask` application and define a route that returns a JSON response. The `index` function creates a dictionary with a message key and value, converts it to a JSON string using `json.dumps()`, and returns it as the response.

To run this script, you will need to install the `flask` module using `pip install flask` and then run the script using `python script.py`. This will start a local web server that listens on port 5000 by default. You can access the JSON response by visiting `http://localhost:5000/` in your web browser.

In addition to returning simple JSON responses, we can also return more complex JSON data structures, such as nested objects and arrays. Here is an example that returns a list of users in JSON format:

```python
import json
from flask import Flask
```

```python
app = Flask(_name_)

@app.route('/users') def users():
users = [
{'id': 1, 'name': 'Alice'},
{'id': 2, 'name': 'Bob'},
{'id': 3, 'name': 'Charlie'}
]
return json.dumps(users)

if____name_== '__main_':
app.run()
```

In this script, the `users` function creates a list of dictionaries, each representing a user with an id and a name. The list is then converted to a JSON string using `json.dumps()` and returned as the response when the `/users` route is accessed.

By returning JSON responses with Python, we can easily communicate data between a server and a client application. JSON is a widely supported format that is easy to work with in many programming languages and frameworks. Python's built-in support for JSON makes it simple to convert Python objects to JSON and back, allowing us to create APIs and web services that return structured data in a standardized format.

In conclusion, returning JSON responses with Python is a common task in web development and data processing. By using the `json` module in Python, we can easily convert Python objects to JSON strings and return them as responses to HTTP requests. This allows us to create APIs and web services that communicate data in a standardized format that is easy to parse and work with. Whether you are building a simple web application or a complex data processing pipeline, Python's support for JSON makes it a powerful tool for working with structured data.

Django Rest Framework with python - scripts

Django Rest Framework is a powerful and flexible toolkit for building Web APIs in Python. It allows you to easily create RESTful APIs with minimal code, making it a popular choice for developers who want to build APIs quickly and efficiently.

In this article, we will explore how to use Django Rest Framework to build a simple API that allows users to create, read, update, and delete data. We will walk through the process of setting up a Django project, creating models, serializers, views, and URLs, and testing our API using the Django Rest Framework's built-in tools.

To get started, make sure you have Django and Django Rest Framework installed on your system. You can install them using pip by running the following commands:

```
pip install django
pip install djangorestframework
```

Once you have Django and Django Rest Framework installed, you can create a new Django project by running the following command:

```
django-admin startproject myproject
```

131

Next, navigate to the project directory and create a new app by running the following command:

```
python manage.py startapp myapp
```

Now, let's define a simple model for our API. Open the `models.py` file in the `myapp` directory and add the following code:

```python
from django.db import models

class Item(models.Model):
name = models.CharField(max_length=100)description =
models.TextField()
price        =        models.DecimalField(max_digits=10,
decimal_places=2)
```

Next, run the following command to create the database tables for our models:

```
python manage.py makemigrations
python manage.py migrate
```

Now, let's create a serializer for our `Item` model. Open the `serializers.py` file in the `myapp` directory and add the following code:

```python
from rest_framework import serializers from
myapp.models import Item

class ItemSerializer(serializers.ModelSerializer):
class Meta:
model = Item
fields = ['id', 'name', 'description', 'price']
```

Next, let's create a view for our API. Open the `views.py`
file in the `myapp` directory and add the followingcode:

```python
from rest_framework import viewsets from myapp.models
import Item
from myapp.serializers import ItemSerializer

class ItemViewSet(viewsets.ModelViewSet):
queryset = Item.objects.all()  serializer_class =
ItemSerializer
```

Now, let's create URLs for our API. Open the `urls.py` file
in the `myapp` directory and add the followingcode:

```python
from django.urls import path, include
from rest_framework.routers import DefaultRouter from
myapp.views import ItemViewSet

router = DefaultRouter()  router.register(r'items',
```

```
ItemViewSet)

urlpatterns = [
path(", include(router.urls)),
]
```

Finally, let's test our API. Run the following command to start the Django development server:

```
python manage.py runserver
```

Now, you can navigate to `http://127.0.0.1:8000/items/` in your web browser to see a list of items in your database. You can also use tools like Postman to test the API endpoints for creating, reading, updating, and deleting items.

We have explored how to use Django Rest Framework to build a simple API in Python. We have created models, serializers, views, and URLs for our API, and tested it using the Django development server. Django Rest Framework is a powerful tool that can help you build robust and efficient APIs with minimal code.

Chapter 12: Introduction to Django Rest Framework

Django Rest Framework (DRF) is a powerful and flexible toolkit for building Web APIs in Django, the popular Python web framework. In this chapter, we will explore the basics of DRF and learn how to create RESTful APIs using Django.

What is Django Rest Framework?

Django Rest Framework is a third-party package that provides a set of tools and libraries for building Web APIs in Django. It is designed to make it easy for developers to create RESTful APIs that adhere to best practices and standards.

DRF provides a number of features that make building APIs in Django easier and more efficient. Some of the key features of DRF include:

Serialization: DRF provides a powerful serialization system that allows you to easily convert complex datatypes, such as Django model instances, into JSON or XML representations that can be easily rendered into HTTP responses.

Authentication: DRF provides a number of built-in authentication classes that make it easy to secure your APIs using token-based authentication, session authentication, or other authentication methods.

Viewsets and Routers: DRF provides a set of powerful tools for defining API endpoints using viewsets and routers. Viewsets allow you to group related views together, while routers automatically generate URL patternsfor your API endpoints.

Permissions: DRF provides a flexible permissions system that allows you to control access to your API endpoints based on user roles and permissions.

Getting Started with Django Rest Framework

To get started with Django Rest Framework, you will first need to install the package using pip. You can do thisby running the following command in your terminal:

```
pip install djangorestframework
```

Once you have installed DRF, you will need to add it to your Django project's list of installed apps in the settings.py file:

```python
INSTALLED_APPS = [
...
'rest_framework',
]
```

Next, you will need to set up DRF's authentication and permission settings in your project's settings.py file. You can do this by adding the following lines to your settings.py file:

```python
REST_FRAMEWORK = {
'DEFAULT_AUTHENTICATION_CLASSES': (
'rest_framework.authentication.TokenAuthentication',
'rest_framework.authentication.SessionAuthentication',
), 'DEFAULT_PERMISSION_CLASSES': (
'rest_framework.permissions.IsAuthenticated',
),
}
```

With DRF installed and configured, you can now start building your API endpoints using DRF's viewsets and routers. To create a new API endpoint, you will first need to define a serializer class that specifies how your data should be serialized into JSON or XML. You can do this by creating a new file called serializers.py in your Django app and defining a serializer class like this:

```python
from rest_framework import serializers from .models import MyModel

class MyModelSerializer(serializers.ModelSerializer):
class Meta:
model = MyModelfields = '_all__'
```

Next, you will need to define a viewset class that specifies how your API endpoint should handle HTTP requests. You can do this by creating a new file called views.py in your Django app and defining a viewset class like this:

```python
from rest_framework import viewsetsfrom .models import MyModel
from .serializers import MyModelSerializer

class MyModelViewSet(viewsets.ModelViewSet):
queryset = MyModel.objects.all() serializer_class = MyModelSerializer
```

Finally, you will need to register your viewset with a router class that automatically generates URL patterns for your API endpoints. You can do this by creating a new file called urls.py in your Django app and defining a router class like this:

```python
from rest_framework.routers import DefaultRouter from
.views import MyModelViewSet

router = DefaultRouter() router.register(r'mymodels',
MyModelViewSet)

urlpatterns = router.urls
```

With your serializer, viewset, and router classes defined,
you can now run your Django project and access your API
endpoints using a web browser or a tool like Postman.
DRF makes it easy to build powerful and flexible APIs in
Django, and with a little practice, you can create APIs that
meet the needs of your users and clients.

We have introduced Django Rest Framework and
explored some of its key features and capabilities. DRF
provides a powerful set of tools and libraries for building
Web APIs in Django, and with a little practice, you can
create RESTful APIs that adhere to best practices and
standards.

By following the steps outlined in this chapter, you can get
started with Django Rest Framework and begin building
your own APIs in Django. Whether you are building a
simple API for a personal project or a complex API for a
large application, DRF provides the tools you need to
create APIs that are secure, efficient, and easy to use.

Setting Up a DRF Project in APIs

Setting up a Django Rest Framework (DRF) project for APIs can be a daunting task for beginners, but with the right guidance and resources, it can be a smooth and rewarding process. In this article, we will walk you through the steps of setting up a DRF project for APIs in Python.

Before we dive into the technical details, let's first understand what DRF is and why it is a popular choice for building APIs in Python. Django Rest Framework is a powerful and flexible toolkit for building Web APIs in Django, which is a high-level Python web framework. DRF provides a set of tools and functionalities that make it easier to build APIs in Django, such as serialization, authentication, permissions, and more.

Now, let's get started with setting up a DRF project for APIs in Python. Here are the steps you need to follow:Step 1: Install Django and Django Rest Framework
The first step is to install Django and Django Rest Framework. You can install them using pip, which is the package installer for Python. Open your terminal and run the following commands:

```
pip install django
pip install djangorestframework
```

Step 2: Create a Django project

Once you have installed Django and DRF, you can create a new Django project using the following command:

```
django-admin startproject myproject
```

This will create a new Django project with the name "myproject". Navigate to the project directory by running:

```
cd myproject
```

Step 3: Create a Django app

Next, you need to create a Django app within the project. Apps are the building blocks of a Django project and contain the logic for specific functionalities. You can create a new app using the following command:

```
python manage.py startapp myapp
```

Replace "myapp" with the name of your app. This will create a new app within the project directory.

Step 4: Configure settings.py

Open the settings.py file in your project directory and add

'rest_framework' to the INSTALLED_APPS list. Thiswill enable DRF in your project. Your INSTALLED_APPS should look like this:

```
INSTALLED_APPS = [

...
'rest_framework','myapp',
]
```

Step 5: Create a model

Now, let's create a model for your app. Models define the structure of your database tables. Open the models.pyfile in your app directory and define a simple model like this:

```
from django.db import models

class MyModel(models.Model):
name = models.CharField(max_length=100)description = models.TextField()
```

Don't forget to run migrations to create the database tables for your model:

```
python manage.py makemigrations python manage.py migrate
```

Step 6: Create a serializer

Serializers are used to convert complex data types, such as querysets and model instances, into native Python datatypes that can be easily rendered into JSON, XML, or other content types. Create a serializer for your model in a new file called serializers.py in your app directory:

```
```

from rest_framework import serializers from myapp.models import MyModel

class MyModelSerializer(serializers.ModelSerializer): class Meta:
model = MyModel

fields = '____all____'
```

Step 7: Create views

Views are the functions that handle HTTP requests and return HTTP responses. Create views for your API in a new file called views.py in your app directory:

```
from rest_framework import viewsets from myapp.models import MyModel
from myapp.serializers import MyModelSerializer

class MyModelViewSet(viewsets.ModelViewSet):
queryset = MyModel.objects.all() serializer_class = MyModelSerializer
```

Step 8: Register the views

Finally, you need to register the views in your project's urls.py file. Open the urls.py file in your project directory and add the following code:

```
from django.urls import path, include
from rest_framework.routers import DefaultRouter from myapp.views import MyModelViewSet

router = DefaultRouter() router.register(r'mymodel', MyModelViewSet)
```
```

```
urlpatterns = [
path(", include(router.urls)),
]
```
```

Step 9: Test your API

Congratulations! You have successfully set up a DRF project for APIs in Python. Now, you can test your API by running the development server:

```

python manage.py runserver
```

Open your browser and navigate to http://127.0.0.1:8000/mymodel/ to see your API in action. You should see a list of objects from your database table.
```

Routing and Serialization for APIs with python

Routing and serialization are two important concepts when it comes to building APIs in Python. In this article, we will discuss what routing and serialization are, why they are important, and how to implement them in yourPython API.

Routing is the process of mapping URLs to specific functions or resources in your API. When a client makes a request to your API, the request is typically sent to a specific URL endpoint. The routing mechanism in your API is responsible for determining which function or resource should handle the request based on the URL provided by the client.

In Python, you can use a variety of libraries to implement routing in your API, such as Flask, Django, or FastAPI. These libraries provide easy-to-use tools for defining URL endpoints and mapping them to specific functions or resources in your API.

For example, in Flask, you can define a route using the `@app.route` decorator, like this:

```python
from flask import Flaskapp = Flask(____name_)
@app.route('/hello')  def hello():
return 'Hello, World!'
```

In this example, the `/hello` URL endpoint is mapped to the `hello` function, which returns the string 'Hello, World!' when the endpoint is accessed by a client.

Serialization, on the other hand, is the process of converting complex data structures, such as Python objects or dictionaries, into a format that can be easily transmitted over the network, such as JSON or XML. When building APIs, it is important to serialize data before sending it to clients and deserialize data received from clients before processing it in your API.

Python provides built-in libraries for serializing and deserializing data, such as the `json` module. You can use this module to convert Python objects or dictionaries into JSON strings and vice versa.

For example, you can serialize a Python dictionary into a JSON string like this:

```python
import json

data = {'name': 'John', 'age': 30}
json_string = json.dumps(data)
print(json_string)
```

This will output `{"name": "John", "age": 30}`, which is a JSON representation of the `data` dictionary. To deserialize a JSON string back into a Python dictionary, you can do this:

```python
json_string = '{"name": "John", "age": 30}' data = json.loads(json_string)
print(data)
```

This will output `{'name': 'John', 'age': 30}`, which is the original Python dictionary that was serialized into the JSON string.

When building APIs, you will often need to combine routing and serialization to handle incoming requests and send responses back to clients. Let's take a look at how you can do this in a Python API using Flask.

First, let's define a simple API endpoint that returns a list of users in JSON format:

```python
from flask import Flask, jsonifyapp = Flask(__name_)
users = [
{'id': 1, 'name': 'Alice'},
{'id': 2, 'name': 'Bob'},
{'id': 3, 'name': 'Charlie'}
]

@app.route('/users')  def get_users():
return jsonify(users)
```

```
if____name_== '__main_':
app.run()
```

In this example, we have defined a list of users and created a `/users` endpoint that returns this list of users in JSON format using the `jsonify` function provided by Flask.

When a client makes a GET request to the `/users` endpoint, the API will serialize the `users` list into a JSON string and send it back to the client as the response.

You can test this API by running the Python script and accessing the `/users` endpoint in your web browser or using a tool like cURL.
Routing and serialization are essential components of building APIs in Python. By properly implementing routing, you can map URL endpoints to specific functions or resources in your API, while serialization allowsyou to convert complex data structures into a format that can be easily transmitted over the network.

In addition to Flask, Django, and FastAPI, there are other Python libraries and frameworks that you can use to build APIs with routing and serialization capabilities, such as Tornado, Bottle, and Falcon. Each of these libraries has its own strengths and weaknesses, so it is important to choose the one that best fits your project requirements.

When implementing routing in your API, make sure to follow best practices, such as using meaningful URL endpoints, handling different HTTP methods (GET, POST, PUT, DELETE), and validating user input to prevent security vulnerabilities.

Similarly, when serializing data in your API, make sure to use a consistent format, such as JSON or XML, and handle errors gracefully if data cannot be serialized or deserialized properly.

Chapter 13: Building APIs with Django Rest Framework

Building APIs (Application Programming Interfaces) has become an essential part of web development. APIs allow different software systems to communicate with each other, enabling the seamless exchange of data and functionality. In this chapter, we will explore how to build APIs using Django Rest Framework, a powerful toolkit for building web APIs in Django.

Django Rest Framework (DRF) is a popular third-party package for Django that simplifies the process of building APIs. It provides a set of tools and functionalities that make it easy to create RESTful APIs with Django. DRF is built on top of Django and leverages its features to provide a robust and flexible framework for building APIs.

To get started with Django Rest Framework, you first need to install the package. You can do this by adding 'rest_framework' to the INSTALLED_APPS setting in your Django project's settings.py file. Once you have installed DRF, you can start building APIs by creating serializers, views, and URLs.

Serializers are a key component of Django Rest Framework. They are used to convert complex data types, such as querysets and model instances, into native Python data types that can be easily rendered into JSON, XML, or other content types. Serializers also handle

151

deserialization, allowing incoming data to be converted back into complex data types.

To create a serializer in Django Rest Framework, you need to define a class that inherits from the Serializer class provided by DRF. You then define the fields that you want to include in the serializer, along with any validation rules or custom logic that you need to apply. Serializers can be used in views to serialize and deserialize data, making it easy to work with complex data structures in your API.

Views in Django Rest Framework are similar to Django views, but with added functionality for working with APIs. DRF provides a set of generic views that can be used to perform common actions, such as listing, creating, updating, and deleting objects. These generic views can be customized to suit your specific requirements, making it easy to build APIs with minimal code.

URLs in Django Rest Framework are used to map API endpoints to views. You can define URLs for different resources in your API, specifying the view that should be used to handle requests to each endpoint. DRF provides a set of tools for defining URLs, including routers that can automatically generate URL patterns based on the views in your API.

In addition to serializers, views, and URLs, Django Rest Framework also provides authentication and permission classes that can be used to secure your API. Authentication classes are used to verify the identity of users accessing your API, while permission classes are used to control access to different parts of your API based on the user's permissions.

Overall, Django Rest Framework provides a powerful and flexible toolkit for building APIs with Django. By leveraging the features and functionality of DRF, you can quickly and easily create RESTful APIs that enable seamless communication between different software systems. In the next chapter, we will explore how to test and deploy APIs built with Django Rest Framework, ensuring that your APIs are robust, secure, and scalable.

Creating RESTful Endpoints for APIs with python

Creating RESTful endpoints for APIs with Python is a crucial skill for any developer looking to build scalable and efficient web applications. RESTful APIs allow for easy communication between different parts of an application or between different applications, making it easier to build complex systems that are maintainable and scalable.

In this article, we will explore how to create RESTful endpoints for APIs with Python. We will cover the basics of RESTful architecture, how to set up a Python environment for building APIs, and how to create endpoints for handling different types of requests.

What is RESTful Architecture?

REST, which stands for Representational State Transfer, is an architectural style for designing networked applications. RESTful architecture is based on a few key principles, including:

Resources: In RESTful architecture, everything is a resource. Resources are identified by URIs (Uniform Resource Identifiers) and can be manipulated using standard HTTP methods such as GET, POST, PUT, and DELETE.

Stateless: RESTful APIs are stateless, meaning that each request from a client to a server must contain all the information necessary to understand and process the request. This allows for scalability and fault tolerance in distributed systems.

Uniform Interface: RESTful APIs have a uniform interface, which means that clients can interact with resources in a consistent way. This simplifies the design and implementation of APIs and makes it easier for developers to understand and use them.

Setting up a Python Environment for Building APIs

Before we can start creating RESTful endpoints for APIs with Python, we need to set up a Python environment. The first step is to install Python on your computer. You can download the latest version of Python from the official website and follow the installation instructions.

Once Python is installed, you can use a package manager like pip to install the necessary dependencies for building APIs. Some popular libraries for building RESTful APIs with Python include Flask, Django, and FastAPI. These libraries provide tools and utilities for creating endpoints, handling requests, and managing resources.

Creating Endpoints for Handling Requests

Now that we have set up our Python environment, we can start creating endpoints for handling different types of requests. In this section, we will use the Flask library to create a simple RESTful API with Python.

First, we need to install Flask using pip:

```
pip install Flask
```

Next, we can create a new Python file and import the Flask library:

```
from flask import Flask, request, jsonify

app = Flask(_name_)
```

We can then define a route for our API endpoint and specify the HTTP methods that are allowed:

```
@app.route('/api/resource', methods=['GET', 'POST']) def handle_resource():
if request.method == 'GET':
# Handle GET request
return jsonify({'message': 'GET request received'}) elif request.method == 'POST':
# Handle POST request data = request.get_json()
return jsonify({'message': 'POST request received', 'data': data})
```

In this example, we have created a simple endpoint that handles GET and POST requests to the `/api/resource` URI. When a GET request is received, the endpoint returns a JSON response with a message indicating that the request was received. When a POST request is received, the endpoint extracts the data from the request body and returns a JSON response with the message and data.

Testing the API Endpoint

To test our API endpoint, we can run the Flask application using the following command:

```
FLASK_APP=app.py flask run
```

This will start a development server that listens for incoming requests on port 5000. We can then use a tool likecURL or Postman to send requests to the API endpoint and verify that it is working correctly.

For example, we can send a GET request to the `/api/resource` URI using cURL:

```
curl http://localhost:5000/api/resource
```

This should return a JSON response with the message indicating that the GET request was received. Similarly,we can send a POST request with some data using cURL:

```
curl -X POST -H "Content-Type: application/json" -d '{"key": "value"}' http://localhost:5000/api/resource
```

157

This should return a JSON response with the message and the data that was sent in the POST request.Conclusion
In this article, we have explored how to create RESTful endpoints for APIs with Python. We have covered the basics of RESTful architecture, how to set up a Python environment for building APIs, and how to create endpoints for handling different types of requests.

By following the examples and guidelines provided in this article, you should be able to create your own RESTful APIs with Python and build scalable and efficient web applications. RESTful APIs are a powerful tool for building complex systems that are maintainable and scalable, and mastering the skills required to create them will make you a more versatile and in-demand developer.

Handling Different HTTP Methods with python

Handling different HTTP methods in Python using Flask involves defining routes that correspond to different HTTP methods (GET, POST, PUT, DELETE, etc.). Here's an example of how you can set this up:

Step 1: Install Flask
First, ensure you have Flask installed. You can do this using pip:

bash
Copiar código
pip install flask
Step 2: Create a Flask Application
Create a file called app.py and add the following code to handle different HTTP methods:

python
Copiar código
from flask import Flask, jsonify, request

app = Flask(__name__)

# Sample data to act as our database
items = [
    {"id": 1, "name": "Item One", "description": "This is item one"},
    {"id": 2, "name": "Item Two", "description": "This is item two"}
]

```python
# Handle GET request - Retrieve all items
@app.route('/items', methods=['GET'])
def get_items():
    return jsonify(items)

# Handle GET request - Retrieve a specific item by id
@app.route('/items/<int:item_id>', methods=['GET'])
def get_item(item_id):
    item = next((item for item in items if item["id"] ==
item_id), None)
    if item is not None:
        return jsonify(item)
    return jsonify({"error": "Item not found"}), 404

# Handle POST request - Create a new item
@app.route('/items', methods=['POST'])
def create_item():
    new_item = request.get_json()
    new_item["id"] = items[-1]["id"] + 1 if items else 1
    items.append(new_item)
    return jsonify(new_item), 201

# Handle PUT request - Update an existing item
@app.route('/items/<int:item_id>', methods=['PUT'])
def update_item(item_id):
    item = next((item for item in items if item["id"] ==
item_id), None)
    if item is None:
        return jsonify({"error": "Item not found"}), 404
    updated_data = request.get_json()
    item.update(updated_data)
    return jsonify(item)
```

```python
# Handle DELETE request - Delete an item
@app.route('/items/<int:item_id>',
methods=['DELETE'])
def delete_item(item_id):
    global items
    items = [item for item in items if item["id"] != item_id]
    return jsonify({"message": "Item deleted"})

if __name__ == '__main__':
    app.run(debug=True)
```

Step 3: Run the Flask Application

To run your Flask application, execute the following command in your terminal:

```bash
Copiar código
python app.py
```

Explanation

GET /items: Returns a list of all items.

GET /items/<item_id>: Returns a specific item by its ID.

POST /items: Creates a new item with the data provided in the request body.

PUT /items/<item_id>: Updates an existing item with the provided ID using the data in the request body.

DELETE /items/<item_id>: Deletes an item with the specified ID.

Testing the API

You can test the API using tools like Postman or curl commands in the terminal. Here are some examples using curl:

Get all items:

161

```bash
Copiar código
curl http://127.0.0.1:5000/items
```
Get a single item:

```bash
Copiar código
curl http://127.0.0.1:5000/items/1
```
Create a new item:

```bash
Copiar código
curl -X POST -H "Content-Type: application/json" -d
'{"name": "Item Three", "description": "This is item
three"}' http://127.0.0.1:5000/items
```
Update an item:

```bash
Copiar código
curl -X PUT -H "Content-Type: application/json" -d
'{"name": "Updated Item", "description": "Updated
description"}' http://127.0.0.1:5000/items/1
```
Delete an item:

```bash
Copiar código
curl     -X     DELETE     http://127.0.0.1:5000/items/
```

Chapter 14: Returning JSON Responses

In this chapter, we will explore how to return JSON responses from our web applications. JSON, which stands for JavaScript Object Notation, is a lightweight data interchange format that is easy for humans to read and write and easy for machines to parse and generate. JSON has become the de facto standard for data exchange on the web, and most modern web APIs use JSON as their data format.

To return JSON responses from our web applications, we need to understand how to serialize our data into JSON format and how to send that JSON data back to the client. In most web development frameworks, this process is straightforward and can be done with just a few lines of code.

To start, let's look at a simple example of how to return a JSON response in a popular web development framework, such as Django in Python. In Django, we can use the JsonResponse class to return JSON data from our views. Here's an example of how we can return a JSON response in Django:

```python
from django.http import JsonResponse

def my_view(request):
```

```python
data = {
'name': 'John Doe','age': 30,
'email': 'john.doe@example.com'
}
return JsonResponse(data)
```

In this example, we define a view function called `my_view` that returns a JSON response with a dictionary containing some sample data. When the client makes a request to this view, they will receive a JSON responsewith the data serialized in JSON format.

In addition to returning simple JSON responses, we can also return more complex JSON data structures, such as lists of dictionaries or nested JSON objects. Here's an example of how we can return a more complex JSON response in Django:

```python
from django.http import JsonResponse

def my_view(request):
data = [
{
'name': 'John Doe','age': 30,
'email': 'john.doe@example.com'
},
{

'name': 'Jane Smith','age': 25,
'email': 'jane.smith@example.com'
}
```

164

```
]
return JsonResponse(data, safe=False)
```

In this example, we define a view function called `my_view` that returns a JSON response with a list of dictionaries containing sample data for two users. We set the `safe` parameter to `False` to allow returning non-dict objects, such as lists.

Returning JSON responses is not limited to Django or Python – most web development frameworks and programming languages have built-in support for serializing data into JSON format. For example, in Node.js with Express, we can use the `res.json()` method to return JSON responses:

```javascript
app.get('/api/users', (req, res) => {const users = [
{    name:    'John    Doe',    age:    30,    email:
'john.doe@example.com' },
{    name:    'Jane    Smith',    age:    25,    email:
'jane.smith@example.com' }
];
res.json(users);
});
```

In this example, we define a route that returns a JSON response with a list of user objects. When the client makes a GET request to this route, they will receive a JSON response with the data serialized in JSON format.

Returning JSON responses is essential for building modern web applications, especially when working with webAPIs that communicate with clients or other services. JSON provides a standardized way to exchange data and is widely supported by web browsers and programming languages.

Returning JSON responses is a fundamental skill for web developers, and understanding how to serialize data into JSON format and send that data back to the client is crucial for building robust and efficient web applications. By mastering the techniques covered in this chapter, you will be well-equipped to handle JSON responses in your web development projects.

Setting Up SQLAlchemy

Setting up SQLAlchemy with Flask involves several steps. SQLAlchemy is a powerful ORM (Object-Relational Mapper) that allows you to interact with your database using Python objects and methods instead of writing raw SQL queries.

Step 1: Install Flask and SQLAlchemy
First, you need to install Flask and SQLAlchemy. You can do this using pip:

```
bash
Copiar código
pip install flask sqlalchemy flask_sqlalchemy
```

Step 2: Set Up the Flask Application with SQLAlchemy
Create a file called app.py and set up your Flask application to use SQLAlchemy:

```python
python
Copiar código
from flask import Flask, jsonify, request
from flask_sqlalchemy import SQLAlchemy

app = Flask(__name__)

# Configuration for the SQLite database
app.config['SQLALCHEMY_DATABASE_URI'] = 'sqlite:///items.db'
app.config['SQLALCHEMY_TRACK_MODIFICATIONS'] = False
```

```python
# Initialize the database
db = SQLAlchemy(app)

# Define the Item model
class Item(db.Model):
    id = db.Column(db.Integer, primary_key=True)
    name = db.Column(db.String(80), nullable=False)
    description = db.Column(db.String(200), nullable=True)

    def to_dict(self):
        return {"id": self.id, "name": self.name, "description": self.description}

# Create the database tables
with app.app_context():
    db.create_all()

# Route to get all items
@app.route('/items', methods=['GET'])
def get_items():
    items = Item.query.all()
    return jsonify([item.to_dict() for item in items])

# Route to get a single item by id
@app.route('/items/<int:item_id>', methods=['GET'])
def get_item(item_id):
    item = Item.query.get(item_id)
    if item is not None:
        return jsonify(item.to_dict())
    return jsonify({"error": "Item not found"}), 404
```

```python
# Route to create a new item
@app.route('/items', methods=['POST'])
def create_item():
    data = request.get_json()
    new_item             =              Item(name=data['name'],
description=data.get('description'))
    db.session.add(new_item)
    db.session.commit()
    return jsonify(new_item.to_dict()), 201


# Route to update an existing item
@app.route('/items/<int:item_id>', methods=['PUT'])
def update_item(item_id):
    item = Item.query.get(item_id)
    if item is None:
        return jsonify({"error": "Item not found"}), 404
    data = request.get_json()
    item.name = data.get('name', item.name)
    item.description          =            data.get('description',
item.description)
    db.session.commit()
    return jsonify(item.to_dict())


# Route to delete an item
@app.route('/items/<int:item_id>',
methods=['DELETE'])
def delete_item(item_id):
    item = Item.query.get(item_id)
    if item is None:
        return jsonify({"error": "Item not found"}), 404
    db.session.delete(item)
    db.session.commit()
    return jsonify({"message": "Item deleted"})
```

```
if __name__ == '__main__':
    app.run(debug=True)
```
Step 3: Run the Flask Application
To run your Flask application, execute the following command in your terminal:

bash
Copiar código
python app.py
Explanation
Configuration: The SQLALCHEMY_DATABASE_URI configures the SQLite database. You can change this to any other database URI if needed.
Database Initialization: The db.create_all() method creates the database tables based on the defined models.
Model Definition: The Item class defines the database table structure.
Routes: Various routes handle different HTTP methods to perform CRUD operations on the Item model.
Testing the API
You can test the API using tools like Postman or curl commands in the terminal. Here are some examples using curl:

Get all items:

bash
Copiar código
curl http://127.0.0.1:5000/items
Get a single item:

bash

170

Copiar código
curl http://127.0.0.1:5000/items/1
Create a new item:

bash
Copiar código
curl -X POST -H "Content-Type: application/json" -d '{"name": "Item Three", "description": "This is item three"}' http://127.0.0.1:5000/items
Update an item:

bash
Copiar código
curl -X PUT -H "Content-Type: application/json" -d '{"name": "Updated Item", "description": "Updated description"}' http://127.0.0.1:5000/items/1
Delete an item:

bash
Copiar código
curl -X DELETE http://127.0.0.1:5000/items/1
This example demonstrates how to set up SQLAlchemy with Flask to handle database operations, providing a complete solution for creating a RESTful API with database integration.

Modeling Database Tables with python

Here's an example of how to model database tables using SQLAlchemy in a Flask application.

Step 1: Install Flask and SQLAlchemy
First, ensure you have Flask and SQLAlchemy installed. You can do this using pip:

bash
Copiar código
pip install flask sqlalchemy flask_sqlalchemy
Step 2: Set Up the Flask Application with SQLAlchemy
Create a file called app.py and set up your Flask application to use SQLAlchemy:

python
Copiar código
from flask import Flask, jsonify, request
from flask_sqlalchemy import SQLAlchemy

app = Flask(__name__)

Configuration for the SQLite database
app.config['SQLALCHEMY_DATABASE_URI'] = 'sqlite:///example.db'
app.config['SQLALCHEMY_TRACK_MODIFICATIONS'] = False

# Initialize the database
db = SQLAlchemy(app)

```python
# Define the User model
class User(db.Model):
    id = db.Column(db.Integer, primary_key=True)
    username = db.Column(db.String(80), nullable=False,
unique=True)
    email = db.Column(db.String(120), nullable=False,
unique=True)

    def to_dict(self):
        return {"id": self.id, "username": self.username,
"email": self.email}

# Define the Post model
class Post(db.Model):
    id = db.Column(db.Integer, primary_key=True)
    title = db.Column(db.String(200), nullable=False)
    content = db.Column(db.Text, nullable=False)
    user_id = db.Column(db.Integer,
db.ForeignKey('user.id'), nullable=False)
    user = db.relationship('User',
backref=db.backref('posts', lazy=True))

    def to_dict(self):
        return {"id": self.id, "title": self.title, "content":
self.content, "user_id": self.user_id}

# Create the database tables
with app.app_context():
    db.create_all()

# Route to get all users
@app.route('/users', methods=['GET'])
```

```python
def get_users():
    users = User.query.all()
    return jsonify([user.to_dict() for user in users])

# Route to create a new user
@app.route('/users', methods=['POST'])
def create_user():
    data = request.get_json()
    new_user = User(username=data['username'], email=data['email'])
    db.session.add(new_user)
    db.session.commit()
    return jsonify(new_user.to_dict()), 201

# Route to get all posts
@app.route('/posts', methods=['GET'])
def get_posts():
    posts = Post.query.all()
    return jsonify([post.to_dict() for post in posts])

# Route to create a new post
@app.route('/posts', methods=['POST'])
def create_post():
    data = request.get_json()
    new_post = Post(title=data['title'], content=data['content'], user_id=data['user_id'])
    db.session.add(new_post)
    db.session.commit()
    return jsonify(new_post.to_dict()), 201

if __name__ == '__main__':
    app.run(debug=True)
```
Step 3: Run the Flask Application

To run your Flask application, execute the following command in your terminal:

bash

```
python app.py
```

Explanation

Configuration: The SQLALCHEMY_DATABASE_URI configures the SQLite database. You can change this to any other database URI if needed.

Database Initialization: The db.create_all() method creates the database tables based on the defined models.

Model Definitions: The User and Post classes define the database table structures. The User class represents a user, and the Post class represents a blog post, which is related to the User class via a foreign key.

Routes: Various routes handle different HTTP methods to perform CRUD operations on the User and Post models.

Testing the API

You can test the API using tools like Postman or curl commands in the terminal. Here are some examples using curl:

Get all users:

bash
Copiar código

```
curl http://127.0.0.1:5000/users
```

Create a new user:

bash
Copiar código

```
curl -X POST -H "Content-Type: application/json" -d
```

'{"username": "user1", "email": "user1@example.com"}'
http://127.0.0.1:5000/users
Get all posts:

```bash
Copiar código
curl http://127.0.0.1:5000/posts
```
Create a new post:

```bash
Copiar código
curl -X POST -H "Content-Type: application
```

Chapter 15: Using SQLAlchemy for Database Integration

In this chapter, we will explore how to use SQLAlchemy for database integration in our language application. SQLAlchemy is a powerful and flexible ORM (Object-Relational Mapping) library for Python that provides a high-level interface to interact with databases. By using SQLAlchemy, we can easily connect to various database systems, create, read, update, and delete records, and perform complex queries with ease.

Setting up SQLAlchemy

To get started with SQLAlchemy, we first need to install the library using pip:

```
pip install sqlalchemy
```

Next, we need to import the necessary modules in our application:

```python
from sqlalchemy import create_engine, Column, Integer, String from sqlalchemy.ext.declarative import declarative_base
from sqlalchemy.orm import sessionmaker
```

Creating a Database Engine

To connect to a database using SQLAlchemy, we need to create an engine object that represents the database connection. We can do this by specifying the database URL in the create_engine function:

```python
engine       =        create_engine('sqlite:///language.db', echo=True)
```

In this example, we are connecting to a SQLite database named language.db. The echo parameter is set to Trueto enable logging of SQL queries.

Defining a Table

Next, we need to define a table in our database using the declarative_base class. We can create a new class that inherits from this base class and define the table structure using class attributes:

```python
Base = declarative_base()

class Word(Base):
_____tablename__= 'words'


id = Column(Integer, primary_key=True) word = Column(String)
```

```python
language = Column(String)
```

In this example, we are defining a table named words with three columns: id (primary key), word, and language.
Creating a Session
To interact with the database, we need to create a session object using the sessionmaker function:

```python
Session = sessionmaker(bind=engine) session = Session()
```

Now that we have set up the database engine, defined a table, and created a session, we can start using SQLAlchemy to perform database operations.

Inserting Records

To insert a new record into the database, we can create a new instance of the Word class and add it to the session:

```python
new_word = Word(word='hello', language='English')
session.add(new_word)
session.commit()
```

In this example, we are inserting a new word record with the word 'hello' and language 'English' into the words table.

Querying Records

To retrieve records from the database, we can use the query method of the session object:

```python
results = session.query(Word).filter(Word.language == 'English').all() for word in results:
print(word.word)
```

In this example, we are querying all words in the English language and printing them to the console. Updating Records
To update an existing record in the database, we can retrieve the record using the query method, modify its attributes, and commit the changes:

```python
word = session.query(Word).filter(Word.word == 'hello').first()word.language = 'Spanish'
session.commit()
```

In this example, we are updating the language of the word 'hello' to 'Spanish'.Deleting Records
To delete a record from the database, we can retrieve the record using the query method and call the deletemethod on the session object:

```python
word = session.query(Word).filter(Word.word == 'hello').first()session.delete(word)
session.commit()
```

In this example, we are deleting the word record with the word 'hello' from the database.

We have learned how to use SQLAlchemy for database integration in our language application. By setting up a database engine, defining a table, creating a session, and using SQLAlchemy's ORM features, wecan easily interact with databases and perform CRUD operations efficiently. SQLAlchemy provides a powerfuland flexible way to work with databases in Python, making it an essential tool for database integration in language applications.

Performing CRUD Operations in APIs with python

In the world of web development, APIs (Application Programming Interfaces) play a crucial role in allowing different systems to communicate with each other. APIs provide a way for developers to access and manipulate data from a remote server. One common task when working with APIs is performing CRUD operations - Create,Read, Update, and Delete.

In this article, we will explore how to perform CRUD operations in APIs using Python. We will use the popular requests library to make HTTP requests to an API and interact with its resources.

Setting up the Environment

Before we start working with APIs, we need to install the requests library. You can install it using pip by running the following command in your terminal:

```
pip install requests
```

Once the requests library is installed, we can start writing code to interact with APIs.

Making GET Requests

The first CRUD operation we will look at is Read, which involves retrieving data from an API. We can do this by making a GET request to the API endpoint that corresponds to the resource we want to access.

Here's an example of how to make a GET request using the requests library:

```python
import requests

# Make a GET request to a sample API endpoint
response = requests.get('https://jsonplaceholder.typicode.com/posts')

# Print the response content
print(response.json())
```

In this example, we are making a GET request to the JSONPlaceholder API, specifically to the /posts endpoint. The response.json() method returns the JSON data returned by the API, which we can then print or manipulate as needed.

Making POST Requests

Next, let's look at the Create operation, which involves adding new data to an API. We can do this by making a

POST request to the API endpoint that corresponds to the resource we want to create. Here's an example of how to make a POST request using the requests library:

```python
import requests

# Define the data to be sent in the POST request
data = {'title': 'New Post', 'body': 'This is a new post', 'userId': 1}

# Make a POST request to create a new post
response = requests.post('https://jsonplaceholder.typicode.com/posts', json=data)

# Print the response content
print(response.json())
```

In this example, we are making a POST request to the JSONPlaceholder API to create a new post. We define the data to be sent in the request as a dictionary and pass it to the json parameter of the requests.post() method.

Making PUT Requests

The Update operation involves modifying existing data in an API. We can do this by making a PUT request to the API endpoint that corresponds to the resource we want to update.

Here's an example of how to make a PUT request using the requests library:

```python
import requests
```

```
# Define the data to be sent in the PUT request
data = {'title': 'Updated Post', 'body': 'This post has been updated', 'userId': 1}

# Make a PUT request to update an existing post
response = requests.put('https://jsonplaceholder.typicode.com/posts/1', json=data)

# Print the response contentprint(response.json())
```
```

In this example, we are making a PUT request to the JSONPlaceholder API to update an existing post. We define the data to be sent in the request as a dictionary and pass it to the json parameter of the requests.put() method. The URL of the request includes the ID of the post we want to update.

Making DELETE Requests

The Delete operation involves removing data from an API. We can do this by making a DELETE request to the
```

API endpoint that corresponds to the resource we want to delete.

Here's an example of how to make a DELETE request using the requests library:

```python
import requests

# Make a DELETE request to delete an existing post
response = requests.delete('https://jsonplaceholder.typicode.com/posts/1')

# Print the response content
print(response.json())
```

In this example, we are making a DELETE request to the JSONPlaceholder API to delete an existing post. The URL of the request includes the ID of the post we want to delete.

Handling Errors

When working with APIs, it's important to handle errors that may occur during the CRUD operations. The requests library provides a built-in way to check for errors in the response.

Here's an example of how to handle errors when making a GET request:

```python
import requests
```

```python
# Make a GET request to a sample API endpoint
response = requests.get('https://jsonplaceholder.typicode.com/posts/100')

# Check if the request was successful if response.status_code == 200:
print(response.json())else:
print('Error:', response.status_code)
```

Setting Up Django ORM with python

Django is a high-level web framework written in Python that encourages rapid development and clean, pragmatic design. One of the key features of Django is its built-in Object-Relational Mapping (ORM) system, which allows developers to interact with the database using Python objects rather than writing raw SQL queries.In this article, we will explore how to set up and use the Django ORM with Python.

Setting up Django ORM with Python

To get started with Django ORM, you first need to install Django. You can do this using pip, the Python package manager, by running the following command:

pip install Django

Once Django is installed, you can create a new Django project by running the following command:django-admin startproject myproject
This will create a new directory called myproject with the following structure:

myproject/ manage.pymyproject/
_____init__.pysettings.py urls.py wsgi.py

Next, navigate to the myproject directory and create a new Django app by running the following command: python manage.py startapp myapp

This will create a new directory called myapp with the following structure:

myapp/
_____init__.py admin.py apps.py migrations/
_____init__.py models.py tests.py views.py

Now that you have set up your Django project and app, you can start defining models using the Django ORM. Models in Django are Python classes that represent database tables. Each model class corresponds to a table in the database, and each attribute of the model class corresponds to a column in the table.

For example, let's say we want to create a simple model to represent a blog post. We can define the model in the models.py file of our app as follows:

```python
from django.db import models

class Post(models.Model):
    title = models.CharField(max_length=100) content = models.TextField()
    created_at = models.DateTimeField(auto_now_add=True)
```

In this example, we have defined a Post model with three attributes: title, content, and created_at. The title attribute is a CharField with a maximum length of 100 characters, the content attribute is a TextField, and the

189

created_at attribute is a DateTimeField that automatically sets the current date and time when a new instance of the model is created.

Once you have defined your models, you need to create and apply migrations to update the database schema. You can do this by running the following commands:

python manage.py makemigrations python manage.py migrate

The makemigrations command generates a migration file that contains the changes to the database schema, and the migrate command applies the migrations to the database.

Now that your models are set up and the database schema is updated, you can start interacting with the database using the Django ORM. You can create, read, update, and delete records in the database using Python code.

For example, to create a new blog post record in the database, you can do the following:

```python
from myapp.models import Post

post = Post(title='Hello, World!', content='This is my first blog post.')post.save()
```

This code creates a new instance of the Post model with the specified title and content, and then saves it to the database using the save() method.

To retrieve all blog post records from the database, you can do the following:

```python
posts = Post.objects.all()


for post in posts:
print(post.title, post.content)
```

This code retrieves all instances of the Post model from the database using the all() method and then iteratesover each post, printing the title and content.

To update an existing blog post record in the database, you can do the following:

```python
post = Post.objects.get(title='Hello, World!')post.content = 'This is my updated blog post.'post.save()
```

This code retrieves the blog post record with the specified title using the get() method, updates the contentattribute, and then saves the changes to the database.

To delete a blog post record from the database, you can do the following:

```python
post = Post.objects.get(title='Hello, World!')post.delete()
```

```

```

This code retrieves the blog post record with the specified title using the get() method and then deletes it from the database using the delete() method.

In addition to basic CRUD operations, the Django ORM provides a rich set of query methods for filtering, ordering, and aggregating data in the database. You can use these query methods to retrieve specific records from the database based on certain criteria.

For example, to retrieve all blog post records that contain the word 'Hello' in the title, you can do the following:

```python
posts = Post.objects.filter(title__icontains='Hello')

for post in posts: print(post.title, post.content)
```

This code uses the filter()

Chapter 16: introduction Asynchronous Programming with FastAPI

Asynchronous programming is a programming paradigm that allows multiple tasks to run concurrently, improving the performance and responsiveness of applications. In this chapter, we will explore how to implement asynchronous programming with FastAPI, a modern web framework for building APIs with Python.

FastAPI is built on top of Starlette and Pydantic, two powerful libraries for building asynchronous web applications. By leveraging the asynchronous features of FastAPI, developers can create high-performance APIs that can handle a large number of concurrent requests efficiently.

One of the key features of FastAPI is its support for asynchronous programming using Python's async and await keywords. These keywords allow developers to define asynchronous functions that can perform non-blocking I/O operations, such as making network requests or querying a database, without blocking the main thread of execution.

To demonstrate how to use asynchronous programming with FastAPI, let's consider a simple example of an API endpoint that fetches data from an external API and returns the results to the client. We will define an asynchronous function that uses the aiohttp library to make an HTTP request to the external API and await the response before returning the data to the client.

```python
from fastapi import FastAPIimport aiohttp

app = FastAPI()

async def fetch_data(url):
async with aiohttp.ClientSession() as session:
async with session.get(url) as response:
return await response.json()

@app.get("/data") async def get_data():
url = "https://api.example.com/data" data = await fetch_data(url)
return data
```

In this example, the get_data function is defined as an asynchronous endpoint using the async keyword. Inside the function, we call the fetch_data function, which makes an asynchronous HTTP request to the external API using aiohttp. By using the await keyword, we can wait for the response to be received before returning the data to the client.

By utilizing asynchronous programming with FastAPI, developers can create APIs that are highly responsive and can handle a large number of concurrent requests without sacrificing performance. Asynchronous programming allows tasks to run concurrently, making it ideal for applications that require I/O-bound operations, such as network requests or database queries.

In addition to improving performance, asynchronous programming with FastAPI can also simplify the development of complex web applications by allowing developers to write code that is more readable and maintainable. By using async and await keywords, developers can write asynchronous functions that are easier to understand and reason about, leading to more robust and scalable applications.

In the following sections of this chapter, we will explore more advanced topics related to asynchronous programming with FastAPI, such as handling errors, using background tasks, and integrating with external services. By mastering these concepts, developers can take full advantage of FastAPI's asynchronous capabilities and build high-performance APIs that meet the demands of modern web applications.

In conclusion, asynchronous programming with FastAPI is a powerful tool for building high-performance APIs that can handle a large number of concurrent requests efficiently. By leveraging the async and await keywords, developers can write code that is more responsive, scalable, and maintainable, making FastAPI an ideal choice for building modern web applications.

Introduction to FastAPI

FastAPI is a modern web framework for building APIs with Python. It is designed to be fast, easy to use, and highly efficient. FastAPI is built on top of Starlette for the web parts and Pydantic for the data parts. It provides a simple and intuitive way to create APIs that are both easy to develop and performant.

One of the key features of FastAPI is its speed. It is one of the fastest web frameworks available for Python, thanks to its use of asynchronous programming techniques. This allows it to handle a large number of concurrent requests with minimal overhead. FastAPI also benefits from the performance optimizations provided by Starlette, which is a lightweight ASGI framework that is used as the foundation for FastAPI.

Another important feature of FastAPI is its ease of use. It is designed to be simple and intuitive, with a clean and concise syntax that makes it easy to write and understand code. FastAPI uses Python type hints to automatically generate API documentation, making it easy to keep documentation up to date as the code changes. It also includes built-in support for data validation and serialization using Pydantic, which helps to ensure that data is handled correctly and consistently throughout the application.

FastAPI is also highly efficient, thanks to its use of modern Python features such as async/await syntax and type hints.

This allows developers to write code that is both performant and easy to understand, without sacrificing readability or maintainability. FastAPI also includes support for automatic dependency injection, which makes it easy to manage dependencies and reduce boilerplate code.

In addition to its speed, ease of use, and efficiency, FastAPI also includes a number of other features that make it a powerful tool for building APIs. It supports automatic generation of OpenAPI documentation, which can be used to document and test APIs quickly and easily. FastAPI also includes support for authentication and authorization, allowing developers to secure their APIs with minimal effort.

Overall, FastAPI is a modern web framework that is well-suited for building APIs with Python. Its speed, ease of use, and efficiency make it a powerful tool for developers who need to build high-performance APIs quickly and easily. Whether you are building a simple REST API or a complex web application, FastAPI is a great choice for building fast, efficient, and reliable APIs.

Getting Started with FastAPI

To get started with FastAPI, you will need to install the framework and create a new project. You can install FastAPI using pip, the Python package manager, by running the following command:

```
```

pip install fastapi

```
```

Once FastAPI is installed, you can create a new project by creating a new Python file and importing the FastAPI module. Here is a simple example of a FastAPI application that defines a single endpoint that returns a JSON response:

```python
from fastapi import FastAPI


app = FastAPI()

@app.get("/")
async def read_root():
    return {"message": "Hello, World!"}
```

In this example, we create a new FastAPI application using the FastAPI class. We then define a single endpoint using the `@app.get` decorator, which specifies that the endpoint should respond to GET requests to the root URL ("/"). The `read_root` function is an asynchronous function that returns a JSON response with a message saying "Hello, World!".

To run the FastAPI application, you can use the `uvicorn` ASGI server, which is included with FastAPI. You can start the server by running the following command:

```
uvicorn app:app --reload
```

```
```

This command starts the `uvicorn` server and tells it to run the `app` module (in this case, the Python file containing the FastAPI application) with the `app` instance as the ASGI application. The `--reload` flag tells `uvicorn` to automatically reload the application when changes are made to the code.

Once the server is running, you can access the API by navigating to `http://localhost:8000` in your web browser. You should see a JSON response with the message "Hello, World!" displayed on the page.

Creating API Endpoints with FastAPI

FastAPI makes it easy to create API endpoints by defining functions that handle HTTP requests and return responses. You can define endpoints for different HTTP methods (GET, POST, PUT, DELETE, etc.) and URL paths by using the corresponding decorators provided by FastAPI.

Here is an example of a FastAPI application that defines multiple endpoints for different HTTP methods and URL paths:

```python
from fastapi import FastAPIapp = FastAPI()
@app.get("/")
async def read_root():
return {"message": "Hello, World!"}
```

```python
@app.post("/items/")
async def create_item(item: dict):

return {"item": item}

@app.put("/items/{item_id}")
async def update_item(item_id: int, item: dict): return
{"item_id": item
```

Setting Up a FastAPI Project with python

FastAPI is a modern web framework for building APIs with Python 3.6+ based on standard Python type hints. It is known for its high performance and ease of use, making it a popular choice for developers looking to create fast and efficient APIs.

In this tutorial, we will walk you through the process of setting up a FastAPI project with Python. By the end of this tutorial, you will have a basic understanding of how to create a FastAPI project and start building your own APIs.

Step 1: Install FastAPI

The first step in setting up a FastAPI project is to install the FastAPI library. You can do this by using pip, the Python package manager. Open a terminal and run the following command:

```
```

pip install fastapi
```
```

This will install the FastAPI library on your system, allowing you to start building APIs using FastAPI. Step 2: Install Uvicorn
Uvicorn is a lightning-fast ASGI server implementation, which is used to run FastAPI applications. To install Uvicorn, run the following command in your terminal:

```
pip install uvicorn
```

Step 3: Create a new Python file

Next, create a new Python file for your FastAPI project. You can name this file anything you like, but for this tutorial, we will name it `main.py`. Open your text editor and create a new file with the following content:

```python
from fastapi import FastAPIapp = FastAPI()
@app.get("/")
async def read_root():
return {"Hello": "World"}
```

This code creates a new FastAPI application with a single route that returns a JSON response with the message "Hello, World" when the root URL is accessed.

Step 4: Run the FastAPI application

To run the FastAPI application, use the Uvicorn server. In your terminal, navigate to the directory where your `main.py` file is located and run the following command:

```
uvicorn main:app --reload
```

This command starts the Uvicorn server with your FastAPI application running. The `--reload` flag enables auto-reloading, so any changes you make to your code will be automatically picked up by the server.

Step 5: Access the API

Once the server is running, you can access your API by opening a web browser and navigating to `http://localhost:8000`. You should see the message "Hello, World" displayed on the page, indicating that your FastAPI application is up and running.

Step 6: Create additional routes

To create additional routes in your FastAPI application, you can define new functions with the `@app.get()` decorator. For example, you can add a new route that returns a list of items by modifying your `main.py` file as follows:

```python
from fastapi import FastAPIapp = FastAPI()
```

```
@app.get("/")
async def read_root():
return {"Hello": "World"}

@app.get("/items/") async def read_items():
return {"items": ["item1", "item2", "item3"]}
```

In this code snippet, we added a new route `/items/` that returns a JSON response with a list of items. You can access this route by navigating to `http://localhost:8000/items/` in your web browser.

Step 7: Add query parameters

FastAPI makes it easy to work with query parameters in your API routes. You can define query parameters by adding them as arguments to your route functions. For example, you can modify the `/items/` route to accept a `limit` query parameter as follows:

```python
from fastapi import FastAPIapp = FastAPI()
@app.get("/")
async def read_root():
return {"Hello": "World"}

@app.get("/items/")
async def read_items(limit: int = 10):
return {"items": ["item1", "item2", "item3"][:limit]}
```

In this code snippet, we added a `limit` query parameter to the `/items/` route, which defaults to 10 if not provided. You can access this route with a specific limit by navigating to `http://localhost:8000/items/?limit=5`.

Step 8: Add request body

FastAPI also supports working with request bodies in your API routes. You can define request body models using Pydantic models and pass them as arguments to your route functions. For example, you can modify the `/items/` route to accept a request body containing a list of items as follows:

```python
from fastapi import FastAPI from pydantic import BaseModel

app = FastAPI()

class Item(BaseModel): name: str
price: float
```

```
@app.post("/items/")
async def create_item(item: Item):return item
```

In this code snippet, we defined a

Chapter 17: Integrating Third-Party APIs

In today's digital world, the use of Application Programming Interfaces (APIs) has become increasingly important for software developers. APIs allow different software systems to communicate with each other, enabling the sharing of data and functionality across different platforms. One common use case for APIs is integrating third-party services into your application. This chapter will explore the process of integrating third-party APIs into your language, providing you with the tools and knowledge needed to successfully incorporate external services into your projects.

What is a Third-Party API?

A third-party API is an interface provided by a third-party service that allows developers to access the functionality and data of that service. These APIs are typically provided by companies such as Google, Facebook, Twitter, and Amazon, to name a few. By integrating these APIs into your language, you can leverage the services and features of these companies within your own applications.

Benefits of Integrating Third-Party APIs

There are several benefits to integrating third-party APIs into your language. One of the most significant advantages is the ability to access powerful services and features without having to build them from scratch. For example, by integrating the Google Maps API into your application, you can easily add mapping functionality without having to develop your own mapping solution.

Additionally, integrating third-party APIs can save you time and resources, as you can leverage the expertise and infrastructure of the third-party service provider. This can help you quickly add new features to your application and stay competitive in the rapidly evolving tech landscape.

Another benefit of integrating third-party APIs is the ability to access a wide range of services and features. From social media integration to payment processing and data analytics, there are APIs available for almost any functionality you can imagine. By integrating these APIs into your language, you can create rich, feature-packed applications that provide value to your users.

Challenges of Integrating Third-Party APIs

While there are many benefits to integrating third-party APIs into your language, there are also some challenges to consider. One of the main challenges is ensuring the security and reliability of the third-party service. When you integrate an API into your application, you are essentially granting that service access to your data and potentially your users' data. It is essential to thoroughly vet the third-party service provider and ensure they have robust security measures in place to protect your data.

Another challenge of integrating third-party APIs is managing dependencies and updates. As third-party servicesevolve and release new versions of their APIs, you will need to update your integration to ensure compatibility. This can be time-consuming and may require changes to your codebase. Additionally, if a third-party service provider discontinues their API or changes their pricing structure, it can impact the functionality of your application.

Best Practices for Integrating Third-Party APIs

To successfully integrate third-party APIs into your language, there are several best practices to follow. First, thoroughly research and vet the third-party service provider before integrating their API. Make sure they have a solid track record of reliability and security, and that their API meets your specific needs.

Next, carefully review the documentation provided by the third-party service provider. Understanding how the API works, what endpoints are available, and how to authenticate requests is crucial for a successful integration. Additionally, consider using SDKs or libraries provided by the service provider, as these can streamline the integration process and handle common tasks such as authentication and error handling.

When integrating a third-party API into your language, it is essential to follow best practices for error handling and data validation. Make sure to handle errors gracefully and provide meaningful error messages to users.
Additionally, validate all data coming from the API to ensure it meets your application's requirements and is safe

to use.

Finally, regularly monitor and test your integration to ensure it remains functional and secure. Set up automated tests to check for changes in the API's behavior and regularly review logs and metrics to identify any issues. By following these best practices, you can ensure a smooth and successful integration of third-party APIs into your language.

Integrating third-party APIs into your language can provide a wide range of benefits, from accessing powerful services and features to saving time and resources. However, it is essential to carefully vet third-party service providers, follow best practices for integration, and regularly monitor and test your integration to ensure it remains secure and reliable. By following the guidance provided in this chapter, you can successfully incorporate external services into your projects and create robust, feature-packed applications that provide value to your users.

Finding and Evaluating APIs with python

When it comes to developing software applications, APIs (Application Programming Interfaces) play a crucial role in enabling communication and data exchange between different software systems. In today's digital age, the availability of APIs has grown exponentially, offering developers a wide range of functionalities and services to integrate into their applications. Python, being a popular programming language, provides developers with powerful tools and libraries to easily work with APIs.

In this article, we will explore how to find and evaluate APIs using Python. We will discuss the different methods and tools available for discovering APIs, as well as techniques for evaluating the quality and reliability of an API. By the end of this article, you will have a better understanding of how to leverage Python to work with APIs effectively.

Finding APIs with Python

There are several ways to discover APIs that are available for integration into your applications. Here are some common methods to find APIs using Python:

API Directories: There are many online directories that list a wide range of APIs available for developers to use. Some popular API directories include ProgrammableWeb, RapidAPI, and APIs.io. These directories provide search functionality to help you find APIs based on specific categories, tags, or keywords.

To search for APIs using Python, you can use web scraping techniques with libraries such as BeautifulSoup or Scrapy. By scraping API directories, you can extract information about different APIs, including their endpoints, documentation, and usage examples.

Social Media and Forums: Developers often share information about APIs on social media platforms like Twitter, LinkedIn, and Reddit. By following relevant hashtags and communities, you can discover new APIs that are being discussed or recommended by other developers.

You can use Python libraries like tweepy or praw to interact with social media APIs and extract information about APIs shared by the community. By monitoring discussions and feedback, you can identify APIs that are popular or highly recommended by other developers.

GitHub Repositories: Many developers publish their APIs on GitHub as open-source projects. By searching GitHub repositories using keywords related to APIs, you can find libraries, SDKs, and code samples that provide access to various APIs.

You can use the GitHub API with Python libraries like requests or PyGithub to search for repositories containing APIs. By analyzing the code and documentation in these repositories, you can evaluate the quality and functionality of the APIs they provide.

API Documentation: Most APIs have official

documentation that describes how to use the API, its endpoints, parameters, and response formats. By exploring API documentation, you can understand the capabilities and limitations of an API before integrating it into your application.

You can use Python libraries like requests or urllib to interact with API endpoints and retrieve data from the API. By making sample requests and analyzing the responses, you can test the functionality and performance of the API.

Evaluating APIs with Python

Once you have identified potential APIs for integration, it is essential to evaluate them based on various criteria to ensure they meet your requirements. Here are some factors to consider when evaluating APIs using Python:

Authentication and Authorization: Many APIs require authentication to access their endpoints securely. You should check the authentication mechanisms supported by the API, such as API keys, OAuth tokens, or JWT tokens. By implementing authentication in your Python code, you can ensure secure communication with the API.

You can use Python libraries like requests-oauthlib or requests-jwt to handle authentication and authorization with OAuth or JWT tokens. By following the API documentation, you can configure the authentication parameters and headers required to access the API endpoints.

Rate Limits and Quotas: APIs often impose rate limits and quotas to control the number of requests a client can make within a specific time period. You should review the rate limit policies of the API to avoid exceeding the allowed limits and getting blocked.

You can use Python libraries like requests or ratelimit to manage rate limits and quotas when making API requests. By monitoring the rate limit headers in API responses, you can track the remaining quota and adjust your request frequency accordingly.

Error Handling: APIs can return various types of errors, such as 4xx client errors or 5xx server errors, in response to invalid requests or server-side issues. You should handle these errors gracefully in your Python code to provide meaningful feedback to users and prevent application crashes.

You can use Python libraries like requests or httpx to handle HTTP errors and exceptions when interacting with APIs. By checking the status codes and error messages in API responses, you can identify the cause of the error and take appropriate actions to recover from it.

Data Formats and Serialization: APIs often use different data formats, such as JSON, XML, or CSV, to represent the data exchanged between clients and servers. You should ensure that your Python code can parse and serialize data in the format expected by the API endpoints.

You can use Python libraries like json or xml.etree.ElementTree to parse and serialize data in

JSON or XML format when working with APIs.

Introduction to GraphQL

GraphQL is a query language for APIs and a runtime for executing those queries by using a type system you define for your data. It allows clients to request only the data they need and nothing more. This is different from traditional REST APIs where clients might get more data than necessary or require multiple requests to different endpoints to get all the required information.

Key Concepts of GraphQL

Schema: A schema defines the types of data and the queries that can be made against the data.

Queries: A query is a read operation that allows clients to request specific fields and nested relationships.

Mutations: Mutations are write operations that allow clients to modify server-side data.

Resolvers: Resolvers are functions that handle the logic for fetching the data for specific types and fields in the schema.

Types: Types are the building blocks of a schema and define the structure of data.

Setting Up GraphQL with Python Using Graphene
Graphene is a library for building GraphQL APIs in Python. Below is an example of how to set up a basic GraphQL API using Flask and Graphene.

Step 1: Install Flask and Graphene
First, ensure you have Flask and Graphene installed. You can do this using pip:

bash

```
pip install flask graphene flask-graphql
```
Step 2: Set Up the Flask Application with Graphene
Create a file called app.py and set up your Flask application to use Graphene:

python
Copiar código
```python
from flask import Flask
from flask_graphql import GraphQLView
import graphene

# Define the User type
class User(graphene.ObjectType):
    id = graphene.ID()
    username = graphene.String()
    email = graphene.String()

# Define a Query type
class Query(graphene.ObjectType):
    users = graphene.List(User)

    def resolve_users(self, info):
        # Dummy data for example purposes
        return [
            User(id="1", username="user1", email="user1@example.com"),
```

```
        User(id="2",                    username="user2",
email="user2@example.com")
    ]

# Define the schema
schema = graphene.Schema(query=Query)

# Create the Flask app
app = Flask(__name__)

# Add GraphQL endpoint
app.add_url_rule(
    '/graphql',
    view_func=GraphQLView.as_view('graphql',
schema=schema, graphiql=True)
)

if __name__ == '__main__':
    app.run(debug=True)
```

Explanation

User Type: The User class defines a GraphQL type with id, username, and email fields.

Query Type: The Query class defines a query type that includes a users field, which returns a list of users.

Schema: The schema ties together the query type.

GraphQL Endpoint: The /graphql endpoint is added to the Flask app, enabling the GraphiQL interface for testing queries.

Step 3: Run the Flask Application

To run your Flask application, execute the following command in your terminal:

Bash

python app.py

Testing the GraphQL API

Once your application is running, you can open your browser and navigate to http://127.0.0.1:5000/graphql. You will see the GraphiQL interface, where you can test your GraphQL queries.

Example Query
In the GraphiQL interface, you can run the following query to get the list of users:

```graphql
Copiar código
{
  users {
   id
   username
   email
  }
}
```

Example Mutation
To handle mutations, you need to define a mutation type. Here's an example to add a user:

```python
python
Copiar código
# Define the User input type
class UserInput(graphene.InputObjectType):
    username = graphene.String(required=True)
    email = graphene.String(required=True)

# Define a mutation for creating a user
class CreateUser(graphene.Mutation):
    class Arguments:
        input = UserInput(required=True)

    user = graphene.Field(lambda: User)

    def mutate(self, info, input):
        user = User(id="3", username=input.username, email=input.email)
        # Here you would typically add the user to your database
        return CreateUser(user=user)

# Update the Mutation class
class Mutation(graphene.ObjectType):
    create_user = CreateUser.Field()

# Update the schema to include mutations
schema = graphene.Schema(query=Query, mutation=Mutation)
```

You can now add the mutation to your GraphiQL interface and run the following mutation:

graphql

Copiar código

```
mutation {
  createUser(input:    {username:    "user3",    email:
"user3@example.com"}) {
    user {
      id
      username
      email
    }
  }
}
```

Chapter 18:Making API Requests in Python

In this chapter, we will explore how to make API requests in Python. APIs, or Application Programming Interfaces, allow different software applications to communicate with each other. They provide a way for developers to access the functionality of a remote service or application.

There are many different types of APIs, including web APIs, which allow developers to interact with web services such as social media platforms, e-commerce websites, and weather data providers. In this chapter, we will focus on how to make HTTP requests to web APIs using Python.

Python provides several libraries that make it easy to work with APIs. One of the most popular libraries for making API requests in Python is the `requests` library. The `requests` library allows you to send HTTP requests to web servers and receive responses in a simple and straightforward way.

To use the `requests` library, you first need to install it using pip, the Python package manager. You can install the `requests` library by running the following command in your terminal:

```
pip install requests
```

Once you have installed the `requests` library, you can start making API requests in Python. The `requests` library provides several functions for sending different types of HTTP requests, such as GET, POST, PUT, DELETE, and PATCH requests.

To make a GET request to a web API using the `requests` library, you can use the `requests.get()` function. For example, to make a GET request to the GitHub API to retrieve information about a specific user, you can use the following code:

```python
import requests

response = requests.get('https://api.github.com/users/octocat')
print(response.json())
```

In this code snippet, we first import the `requests` library and then use the `requests.get()` function to send a GET request to the GitHub API to retrieve information about the user with the username `octocat`. The `response.json()` function is used to parse the JSON response from the API and print it to the console.

In addition to making GET requests, you can also make POST requests to web APIs using the `requests` library. POST requests are commonly used to send data to a web server, such as submitting a form or creating a new resource.

To make a POST request to a web API using the `requests` library, you can use the `requests.post()` function. For example, to create a new user on a hypothetical user management API, you can use the following code:

```python
import requests

data = {'username': 'john_doe', 'email': 'john.doe@example.com'}
response = requests.post('https://api.example.com/users', json=data)
print(response.json())
```

In this code snippet, we first define a dictionary `data` containing the user information that we want to send to the API. We then use the `requests.post()` function to send a POST request to the hypothetical user management API with the user data in JSON format. The `response.json()` function is used to parse the JSON response from the API and print it to the console.

In addition to making GET and POST requests, the `requests` library also provides functions for making PUT, DELETE, and PATCH requests to web APIs. PUT requests are commonly used to update existing resources on a web server, while DELETE requests are used to delete resources. PATCH requests are used to partially update a resource on a web server.

To make a PUT request to a web API using the `requests` library, you can use the `requests.put()` function. For example, to update the email address of a user on a

224

hypothetical user management API, you can use the following code:

```python
import requests

data = {'email': 'john.doe.updated@example.com'}
response = requests.put('https://api.example.com/users/john_doe', json=data)
print(response.json())
```

In this code snippet, we first define a dictionary `data` containing the updated email address for the user. We then use the `requests.put()` function to send a PUT request to the hypothetical user management API with the updated user data in JSON format. The `response.json()` function is used to parse the JSON response from the API and print it to the console.

To make a DELETE request to a web API using the `requests` library, you can use the `requests.delete()` function. For example, to delete a user from a hypothetical user management API, you can use the following code:

```python
import requests

response = requests.delete('https://api.example.com/users/john_doe')
print(response.json())
```

In this code snippet, we use the `requests.delete()` function to send a DELETE request to the hypothetical user management API to delete the user with the username `john_doe`.

Introduction to the Requests Library

The Requests library in Python is a powerful tool for making HTTP requests in a simple and user-friendly way. It is widely used in web development and data science projects for fetching data from APIs, scraping websites, and interacting with web services. In this article, we will introduce you to the Requests library and show you how to use it to make HTTP requests in Python.

What is the Requests Library?

The Requests library is an open-source Python library that allows you to send HTTP requests easily. It provides a simple and elegant API for making HTTP requests and handling responses. With the Requests library, you can make GET, POST, PUT, DELETE, and other types of HTTP requests with just a few lines of code.

The Requests library is built on top of the urllib3 library, which provides a low-level interface for making HTTP requests in Python. However, the Requests library simplifies the process of making HTTP requests by providing a higher-level API that is more user-friendly and intuitive.

Installing the Requests Library

Before you can start using the Requests library, you need to install it on your system. You can install the Requests library using pip, the Python package manager. To install

227

the Requests library, open a terminal or command prompt and run the following command:

```
pip install requests
```

This will download and install the Requests library on your system. Once the installation is complete, you can start using the Requests library in your Python scripts.

Making a GET Request

To make a GET request using the Requests library, you can use the `requests.get()` function. This function takes a URL as an argument and returns a `Response` object that contains the response from the server. Here's an example of how to make a GET request using the Requests library:

```
import requests

url = 'https://jsonplaceholder.typicode.com/posts/1'
response = requests.get(url)

print(response.text)
```

In this example, we are making a GET request to the JSONPlaceholder API to fetch a post with the ID of 1. The `response.text` attribute contains the response body as a string, which we are printing to the console.

Handling Response Status Codes

When you make an HTTP request using the Requests library, the server will send back a response with a status code that indicates the outcome of the request. The status code is a three-digit number that provides information about the success or failure of the request. Here are some common HTTP status codes:

200: OK - The request was successful.
400: Bad Request - The request was malformed or invalid.
404: Not Found - The requested resource was not found.
500: Internal Server Error - The server encountered an error while processing the request.

You can access the status code of the response using the `response.status_code` attribute. Here's an example of how to check the status code of a response:

```
` ` `

import requests

url = 'https://jsonplaceholder.typicode.com/posts/1'
response = requests.get(url)

if response.status_code == 200:
print('Request was successful')else:
print('Request failed with status code:', response.status_code)
` ` `
```

In this example, we are checking the status code of the

response and printing a message based on the outcome of the request.

Handling Response Headers

In addition to the response body and status code, the server may also send back headers with the response. Response headers contain metadata about the response, such as the content type, content length, and encoding. You can access the response headers using the `response.headers` attribute, which returns a dictionary of header key-value pairs. Here's an example of how to access the response headers:

```
import requests

url = 'https://jsonplaceholder.typicode.com/posts/1'
response = requests.get(url)

print(response.headers)
```

In this example, we are printing the response headers to the console. The headers dictionary contains key-value pairs where the keys are the header names and the values are the header values. Sending Query Parameters
When making a GET request, you can include query parameters in the URL to filter or sort the results returned by the server. You can pass query parameters as a dictionary to the `params` parameter of the `requests.get()` function. Here's an example of how to send query parameters in a GET request:

```
import requests

url = 'https://jsonplaceholder.typicode.com/posts'params
= {'userId': 1}
response = requests.get(url, params=params)

print(response.json())
```

In this example, we are sending a GET request to the JSONPlaceholder API with a query parameter `userId` set to 1. The `response.json()` method parses the response body as JSON and returns a Python object.

Sending POST Requests

In addition to making GET requests, you can also make POST requests using the Requests library. To make a POST request, you can use the `requests.post`

Making GET, POST, PUT, DELETE Requests with python

Python is a versatile programming language that is widely used for web development. One of the key features of Python is its ability to make HTTP requests, such as GET, POST, PUT, and DELETE requests. In this article, we will explore how to make these types of requests using Python.

GET Request:

A GET request is used to retrieve data from a server. In Python, you can make a GET request using the requests library. Here is an example of how to make a GET request in Python:

```python
import requests

url = 'https://jsonplaceholder.typicode.com/posts/1'
response = requests.get(url)

data = response.json()print(data)
```

In this example, we are making a GET request to the JSONPlaceholder API to retrieve a specific post. The response object contains the data returned by the server, which we can access using the json() method.

POST Request:

A POST request is used to send data to a server. In Python, you can make a POST request using the requestslibrary. Here is an example of how to make a POST request in Python:

```python
import requests

url = 'https://jsonplaceholder.typicode.com/posts' data = {'title': 'foo', 'body': 'bar', 'userId': 1} response = requests.post(url, json=data)

data = response.json()print(data)
```

In this example, we are making a POST request to the JSONPlaceholder API to create a new post. The data variable contains the data that we want to send to the server, which is passed to the post() method as a json parameter.

PUT Request:

A PUT request is used to update data on a server. In Python, you can make a PUT request using the requests library. Here is an example of how to make a PUT request in Python:

```python
import requests

url = 'https://jsonplaceholder.typicode.com/posts/1'
data = {'title': 'foo', 'body': 'bar', 'userId': 1}
response = requests.put(url, json=data)

data = response.json()
print(data)
```

In this example, we are making a PUT request to the JSONPlaceholder API to update an existing post. The data variable contains the updated data that we want to send to the server, which is passed to the put() method as a json parameter.

DELETE Request:

A DELETE request is used to delete data from a server. In Python, you can make a DELETE request using the requests library. Here is an example of how to make a DELETE request in Python:

```python
import requests

url = 'https://jsonplaceholder.typicode.com/posts/1'
response = requests.delete(url)

print(response.status_code)
```

In this example, we are making a DELETE request to the JSONPlaceholder API to delete a specific post. The response object contains information about the status of the request, which we can access using the status_code attribute.

In conclusion, Python provides a simple and intuitive way to make HTTP requests using the requests library. By following the examples provided in this article, you can easily make GET, POST, PUT, and DELETE requests in Python for your web development projects.

Chapter 19: Consuming RESTful APIs with Requests

In this chapter, we will discuss how to consume RESTful APIs using the Requests library in Python. RESTful APIs are a popular way for applications to communicate with each other over the internet. They allow developers to send and receive data in a standardized format, making it easier to integrate different systems and services.

The Requests library is a powerful and user-friendly tool for making HTTP requests in Python. It provides a simple and intuitive API for sending and receiving data from web servers, including RESTful APIs. With Requests, you can easily make GET, POST, PUT, DELETE, and other types of HTTP requests, and handle responses in a variety of formats, such as JSON, XML, or plain text.

To get started with Requests, you first need to install the library using pip, Python's package manager. You can do this by running the following command in your terminal or command prompt:

```
pip install requests
```

Once you have installed Requests, you can start using it in your Python code by importing the library at the top of your script:

```python
import requests
```

Now that you have imported the Requests library, you can begin making HTTP requests to consume RESTful APIs. The most common type of request is a GET request, which is used to retrieve data from a server. Here is an example of how to make a GET request using Requests:

```python
response = requests.get('https://api.example.com/data')
```

In this example, we are sending a GET request to the URL 'https://api.example.com/data'. The response object contains the server's response to our request, including the data that we requested. We can access the response data by calling the `json()` method on the response object, which will parse the response as JSON and return it as a Python dictionary:

```python
data = response.json()print(data)
```

This will print the data returned by the API in a human-readable format. Depending on the API you are consuming, the data may be structured in different ways, so you may need to inspect the response object to understand how to access the information you need.

In addition to GET requests, Requests also supports other HTTP methods, such as POST, PUT, and DELETE. These methods are used to create, update, and delete data on the server, respectively. Here is an example of how to make a POST request using Requests:

```python
payload = {'key': 'value'}
response = requests.post('https://api.example.com/data', json=payload)
```

In this example, we are sending a POST request to the URL 'https://api.example.com/data' with a payload containing a key-value pair. The `json` parameter is used to send the payload as JSON data in the request body.

Once you have made a request to a RESTful API, you may need to handle the response in different ways depending on the data format and structure. For example, if the API returns an error response, you may need to handle the error and take appropriate action in your code. Requests provides several methods for checking the status of the response, accessing headers, and handling different types of responses.

Consuming RESTful APIs with Requests in Python is a powerful and flexible way to interact with web services and exchange data between different systems. By using the Requests library, you can easily make HTTP requests, handle responses in various formats, and integrate external APIs into your applications.

Whether you are building a web application, a data processing pipeline, or a machine learning model, Requests can help you communicate with RESTful APIs efficiently and effectively.

Handling Responses and Errors in APIs

When working with APIs, it is important to consider how to handle responses and errors effectively. APIs are used to communicate between different systems and applications, and it is common for errors to occur during this communication process. By understanding how to handle responses and errors in APIs, developers can ensure that their applications are robust and reliable.

One of the key aspects of handling responses and errors in APIs is understanding the different types of responses that can be returned by an API. APIs typically use HTTP status codes to indicate the outcome of a request.
These status codes can be grouped into different categories, such as informational responses (1xx), successful responses (2xx), redirection responses (3xx), client error responses (4xx), and server error responses (5xx.

When a request is made to an API, the API will return a response that includes a status code along with any relevant data. It is important for developers to check the status code of the response in order to determine whether the request was successful or if an error occurred. For example, a status code of 200 indicates that the request was successful, while a status code of 404 indicates that the requested resource was not found.

In addition to checking the status code of the response, developers should also consider the data that is returned by the API. In some cases, the API may return additional information in the response body that can provide more context about the outcome of the request. This data can be used to help developers understand why an error occurred and how to resolve it.

When handling responses in APIs, developers should also consider how to handle pagination. Many APIs return large amounts of data that may need to be paginated in order to improve performance. Developers should be aware of how to handle pagination in order to efficiently retrieve and process large datasets from an API.

In addition to handling responses, developers should also consider how to handle errors in APIs. Errors can occur for a variety of reasons, such as invalid input, authentication issues, or server failures. When an error occurs, the API will typically return an error response that includes a status code along with an error message.

When handling errors in APIs, developers should consider how to communicate these errors to users in a clear and informative way. Error messages should be descriptive and provide users with information about what went wrong and how to resolve the issue. By providing users with helpful error messages, developers can improve the user experience and make it easier for users to troubleshoot problems.

In addition to communicating errors to users, developers should also consider how to handle errors programmatically. When an error occurs, developers should catch the error and handle it appropriately in their code. This may involve logging the error, retrying the request, or taking other corrective actions to address the issue.

One common technique for handling errors in APIs is to use try-catch blocks in the code. By wrapping API calls in a try-catch block, developers can catch any errors that occur and handle them gracefully. This can help prevent the application from crashing and provide a better user experience.

Another important aspect of handling errors in APIs is implementing error handling mechanisms at the API level. APIs should be designed to return informative error responses that include status codes and error messages. By providing clear and consistent error responses, developers can make it easier for clients to understand and respond to errors.

When designing APIs, developers should also consider how to handle rate limiting and throttling. Rate limiting is a common technique used to prevent abuse of an API by limiting the number of requests that can be made within a certain time period. Throttling is similar to rate limiting but involves slowing down the rate of requests rather than blocking them entirely.

By implementing rate limiting and throttling mechanisms in an API, developers can protect the API from being overwhelmed by excessive requests. This can help improve the performance and reliability of the API and ensure that all users have fair access to its resources.

In addition to rate limiting and throttling, developers should also consider how to handle authentication and authorization errors in APIs. Authentication errors occur when a user is not properly authenticated to access a resource, while authorization errors occur when a user is not authorized to perform a certain action. By handling these errors appropriately, developers can ensure that only authorized users are able to access and interact with the API.

Overall, handling responses and errors in APIs is an important aspect of developing reliable and robust applications. By understanding how to check status codes, handle pagination, communicate errors to users, and implement error handling mechanisms, developers can ensure that their applications are able to effectively interact with APIs and provide a seamless user experience. By following best practices for handling responses and errors in APIs, developers can build applications that are more resilient, scalable, and secure.

Chapter 20: Working with GraphQL APIs

Working with GraphQL APIs involves defining your data schema, creating resolvers to handle queries and mutations, and setting up a server to process GraphQL requests. Below is an example of how to work with GraphQL APIs using Flask and Graphene in Python.

Step-by-Step Guide

Install Dependencies: Install Flask and Graphene.

Define Schema: Create a GraphQL schema with types and fields.

Create Resolvers: Implement resolvers to fetch or modify data.

Set Up Flask Server: Integrate GraphQL with Flask.

Test API: Use tools like GraphiQL or Postman to test your API.

Step 1: Install Dependencies

Use pip to install the necessary packages:

bash

```
pip install flask graphene flask-graphql
```

Step 2: Define the Schema

Create a file called app.py and start by defining the schema.

Python

```python
from flask import Flask
from flask_graphql import GraphQLView
import graphene

# Define User type
class User(graphene.ObjectType):
    id = graphene.ID()
    username = graphene.String()
    email = graphene.String()

# Define Query type
class Query(graphene.ObjectType):
    users = graphene.List(User)

    def resolve_users(self, info):
        # Sample data
        return [
            User(id="1",               username="user1",
email="user1@example.com"),
            User(id="2",               username="user2",
email="user2@example.com")
        ]

# Define Mutation to create a user
class CreateUser(graphene.Mutation):
    class Arguments:
```

```python
    username = graphene.String(required=True)
    email = graphene.String(required=True)

  user = graphene.Field(lambda: User)

  def mutate(self, info, username, email):
    user    =    User(id="3",    username=username,
email=email)
    # Here you would typically save the user to the
database
    return CreateUser(user=user)

# Define Mutation type
class Mutation(graphene.ObjectType):
  create_user = CreateUser.Field()

# Create schema
schema    =    graphene.Schema(query=Query,
mutation=Mutation)
```

Step 3: Set Up Flask Server
Integrate the GraphQL schema with Flask and set up the server.

python
Copiar código
```python
# Create Flask app
app = Flask(__name__)

# Add GraphQL endpoint
app.add_url_rule(
  '/graphql',
  view_func=GraphQLView.as_view('graphql',
schema=schema, graphiql=True)
```

```
)

if __name__ == '__main__':
    app.run(debug=True)
```

Step 4: Run the Server
Run the Flask application:

bash

```
python app.py
```

Step 5: Test the API
Once your server is running, navigate to http://127.0.0.1:5000/graphql to access the GraphiQL interface. You can use this interface to test your queries and mutations.

Example Query
Fetch all users:

graphql
Copiar código

```
{
  users {
    id
    username
    email
  }
}
```

Example Mutation
Create a new user:

graphql
Copiar código

```
mutation {
  createUser(username:           "user3",           email:
"user3@example.com") {
    user {
      id
      username
      email
    }
  }
}
```

Adding More Complexity
Define More Types
You can add more types to your schema. For example, let's add a Post type and define a relationship between users and posts.

python
Copiar código

```python
class Post(graphene.ObjectType):
    id = graphene.ID()
    title = graphene.String()
    content = graphene.String()
    user_id = graphene.Int()

class User(graphene.ObjectType):
    id = graphene.ID()
    username = graphene.String()
    email = graphene.String()
    posts = graphene.List(Post)

    def resolve_posts(self, info):
        # Sample posts data
        if self.id == "1":
```

```python
    return [
        Post(id="1", title="First Post", content="Content
of the first post", user_id=1),
        Post(id="2",          title="Second          Post",
content="Content of the second post", user_id=1)
        ]
    else:
        return []

class Query(graphene.ObjectType):
    users = graphene.List(User)
    posts = graphene.List(Post, user_id=graphene.Int())

    def resolve_users(self, info):
        return [
            User(id="1",                    username="user1",
email="user1@example.com"),
            User(id="2",                    username="user2",
email="user2@example.com")
        ]

    def resolve_posts(self, info, user_id):
        # Sample posts data
        if user_id == 1:
            return [
        Post(id="1", title="First Post", content="Content
of the first post", user_id=1),
        Post(id="2",          title="Second          Post",
content="Content of the second post", user_id=1)
        ]
    else:
        return []
```
Example Query with Relationships

Fetch all users and their posts:

```graphql
Copiar código
{
  users {
    id
    username
    email
    posts {
      id
      title
      content
    }
  }
}
```

This example demonstrates the basics of working with GraphQL APIs in Python using Flask and Graphene. You can expand this setup by connecting to a real database, adding authentication, and defining more complex queries and mutations.

Differences Between REST and GraphQL

When it comes to building APIs for web applications, developers have a few different options to choose from. Two of the most popular choices are REST and GraphQL. While both are used to create APIs, they have some key differences that make them better suited for different types of projects.

REST, which stands for Representational State Transfer, is a well-established architectural style for designing networked applications. It relies on a stateless, client-server communication model and uses standard HTTP methods like GET, POST, PUT, and DELETE to perform operations on resources. REST APIs are typically organized around resources, with each resource being represented by a URL. For example, a REST API for a blog might have URLs like /posts, /comments, and /users.

GraphQL, on the other hand, is a newer technology that was developed by Facebook in 2015. It is a query language and runtime for APIs that allows clients to request only the data they need. With GraphQL, clients can specify exactly what data they want to retrieve in their queries, which can help reduce over-fetching and under-fetching of data. This makes GraphQL a more flexible and efficient option for building APIs that need to support a wide range of client requirements.

One of the main differences between REST and GraphQL is how they handle data fetching. In a REST API, each endpoint represents a specific resource, and clients can only request data from that resource by making a separate HTTP request to the corresponding URL. This can lead to issues like over-fetching, where the client receives more data than it needs, or under-fetching, where the client needs to make multiple requests to get all the data it requires.

In contrast, GraphQL allows clients to request exactly the data they need in a single query. Clients can specify the fields they want to retrieve, as well as any related data they need, in a single request to the GraphQL server. This can help reduce the number of requests needed to fetch all the required data, as well as prevent issues like over-fetching and under-fetching.

Another key difference between REST and GraphQL is how they handle versioning. In a REST API, versioning is typically done by adding a version number to the URL of the API endpoint. For example, a REST API might have endpoints like /v1/posts and /v2/posts to represent different versions of the API. This can lead to issues like endpoint proliferation and complexity, as well as potential breaking changes for clients when a new version is released.

GraphQL, on the other hand, does not require versioning in the same way as REST. Because clients can specify exactly what data they need in their queries, changes to the underlying data structure can be made without affecting existing clients. This can make it easier to evolve and maintain GraphQL APIs over time, as changes can be made without breaking existing clients.

One area where REST and GraphQL differ is in how they handle caching. In a REST API, caching is typically done at the HTTP level using mechanisms like ETags and cache control headers. Clients can cache responses from the server based on the resource URL and other cache-related headers, which can help improve performance and reduce server load.

GraphQL, on the other hand, does not have built-in support for caching at the HTTP level. Because each GraphQL query is unique and can request different data, caching responses becomes more challenging.

However, GraphQL servers can implement their own caching mechanisms to store and reuse query results, which can help improve performance and reduce redundant data fetching.

In terms of tooling and ecosystem, REST has a more mature and established ecosystem compared to GraphQL. There are many tools and libraries available for building and consuming REST APIs, as well as well-defined best practices and conventions. This can make it easier for developers to get started with REST and find resources to help them build and maintain their APIs.

GraphQL, on the other hand, is still a relatively new technology, and its ecosystem is not as mature as REST. There are fewer tools and libraries available for GraphQL, and best practices are still evolving. However, GraphQL has gained popularity in recent years, and there are now many resources available to help developers learn how to use GraphQL effectively.

REST and GraphQL are both popular choices for building APIs, but they have some key differences that make them better suited for different types of projects. REST is a well-established architectural style that is good for building APIs that are resource-centric and need to support a wide range of clients.

GraphQL, on the other hand, is a more flexible and efficient option for building APIs that need to support complex data requirements and reduce over-fetching and under-fetching. Ultimately, the choice between REST and GraphQL will depend on the specific requirements of your project and the trade-offs you are willing to make in terms of flexibility, performance, and ease of use.

Consuming GraphQL APIs in Python

There are several libraries available in Python that make this process easier, such as requests and gql. Below, I'll show you examples using both of these libraries.

Using requests Library
The requests library is a popular HTTP library in Python that you can use to send HTTP requests, including GraphQL queries and mutations.

Install requests:

bash
Copiar código
pip install requests
Send GraphQL Queries and Mutations:

python
Copiar código
import requests

# Define the GraphQL endpoint
url = 'http://127.0.0.1:5000/graphql'

# Define a query
query = '''
{
  users {
    id
    username

```
    email
  }
}
"""
```

```python
# Send the request
response = requests.post(url, json={'query': query})

# Print the response
print(response.json())
```

Send a Mutation:

```python
Copiar código
mutation = '''
mutation {
  createUser(username:          "user3",          email:
"user3@example.com") {
    user {
      id
      username
      email
    }
  }
}
'''
```

```python
response = requests.post(url, json={'query': mutation})
print(response.json())
```

Using gql Library

The gql library is a more specialized GraphQL client for
Python.

Install gql:

```bash
Copiar código
pip install gql[requests]
Send GraphQL Queries and Mutations:
```

```python
Copiar código
from gql import gql, Client
from gql.transport.requests import RequestsHTTPTransport

# Define the transport
transport = RequestsHTTPTransport(
    url='http://127.0.0.1:5000/graphql',
    use_json=True,
)

# Create the client
client = Client(
    transport=transport,
    fetch_schema_from_transport=True,
)

# Define a query
query = gql('''
{
  users {
    id
    username
    email
  }
```

```
}
"'")
```

```python
# Execute the query
result = client.execute(query)
print(result)
```

Send a Mutation:

python
Copiar código
```python
mutation = gql("'
mutation {
  createUser(username:          "user3",          email:
"user3@example.com") {
    user {
      id
      username
      email
    }
  }
}
"'")
```

```python
result = client.execute(mutation)
print(result)
```

Handling Responses

The responses from GraphQL APIs are typically JSON objects. Here's an example of how to handle the responses:

python
Copiar código
```python
response = requests.post(url, json={'query': query})
```

```python
data = response.json()

if 'errors' in data:
    print("Errors:", data['errors'])
else:
    print("Data:", data['data'])
```

Example Scenario: Fetching Data from a Public GraphQL API
Let's use the SpaceX GraphQL API as an example.

Install requests (if not already installed):

bash
Copiar código
```bash
pip install requests
```
Send a Query to SpaceX API:

python
Copiar código
```python
import requests

url = 'https://api.spacex.land/graphql/'

query = '''
{
  launchesPast(limit: 3) {
    mission_name
    launch_date_utc
    launch_site {
      site_name_long
    }
    links {
      video_link
```

```
    }
    rocket {
      rocket_name
    }
  }
}
"""

response = requests.post(url, json={'query': query})
data = response.json()

if 'errors' in data:
    print("Errors:", data['errors'])
else:
    print("Data:", data['data'])
```

Consuming GraphQL APIs in Python is straightforward using libraries like requests and gql. You can send queries and mutations to any GraphQL endpoint and handle the responses as JSON. This allows you to integrate GraphQL-based data fetching and mutations into your Python applications seamlessly.

Chapter 21: Building Microservices Architecture

In today's fast-paced and ever-changing world of technology, the need for scalable and flexible software architecture has become more important than ever. This is where microservices architecture comes into play. Microservices architecture is a software development technique that structures an application as a collection of loosely coupled services. These services are highly maintainable and testable, and can be developed, deployed, and scaled independently. In this chapter, we will explore the key concepts and best practices for building a microservices architecture.

One of the main benefits of microservices architecture is its ability to break down complex applications into smaller, more manageable components. Each service is responsible for a specific set of functionalities, which makes the overall system easier to understand and maintain. This also allows for faster development cycles, as teams can work on different services simultaneously without impacting each other.

Another advantage of microservices architecture is its scalability. Since each service is independent, it can be scaled horizontally to handle increased load. This is in contrast to monolithic applications, where scaling often involves adding more resources to the entire application, even if only a small portion of it is under heavy load.

In order to build a successful microservices architecture, there are several key principles that should be followed. First and foremost, services should be loosely coupled. This means that each service should have its own database and communicate with other services through well-defined APIs. This allows for greater flexibility and resilience, as services can be developed, deployed, and scaled independently.

Another important principle is service autonomy. Each service should be responsible for its own data and business logic, and should not depend on other services to perform its functions. This ensures that services can be developed and deployed independently, without impacting other parts of the system.

Additionally, services should be designed with failure in mind. Since microservices architecture relies on distributed systems, failures are inevitable. Services should be able to handle failures gracefully, and should have mechanisms in place for handling errors and retries.

Security is also a critical consideration when building a microservices architecture. Each service should have its own security mechanisms in place, such as authentication and authorization, to ensure that sensitive data is protected. Additionally, communication between services should be encrypted to prevent unauthorized access.

Monitoring and logging are also important aspects of microservices architecture. Each service should have its own monitoring and logging mechanisms in place to track performance metrics, detect issues, and troubleshoot problems. This allows for greater visibility into the system and helps teams quickly identify and resolve issues.

Building a microservices architecture requires careful planning and consideration of key principles and best practices. By following these guidelines, teams can create scalable, flexible, and maintainable systems that can adapt to changing business needs.

Microservices architecture is a powerful tool for modern software development, and when implemented correctly, can lead to faster development cycles, greater scalability, and improved resilience.

Understanding Microservices

Microservices architecture has become increasingly popular in recent years as more and more organizations move towards a more agile and scalable approach to software development. Understanding microservices is crucial for developers, architects, and business stakeholders alike in order to fully leverage the benefits of this architecture style.

What are Microservices?

Microservices are a software development approach that structures an application as a collection of loosely coupled services. Each service is self-contained and performs a specific business function. These services communicate with each other through APIs, allowing for greater flexibility and scalability compared to traditional monolithic architectures.

In a monolithic architecture, the entire application is built as a single unit, with all the code tightly integrated. This can lead to issues such as long development cycles, difficulty in scaling, and a lack of flexibility.
Microservices, on the other hand, break down the application into smaller, more manageable services that can be developed, deployed, and scaled independently.

Key Characteristics of Microservices

There are several key characteristics that define

microservices architecture:

Decentralized Data Management: Each microservice has its own database, which allows for greater autonomy and flexibility. This also helps to prevent data coupling between services.

Independent Deployment: Microservices can be deployed independently of each other, allowing for faster release cycles and easier maintenance.

Resilience: Microservices are designed to be resilient to failures. If one service goes down, it does not bring down the entire application.

Scalability: Microservices can be scaled independently, allowing for better resource utilization and cost efficiency.

Polyglot Development: Microservices can be developed using different programming languages and frameworks, depending on the specific requirements of each service.

Benefits of Microservices

There are several benefits to using a microservices architecture:

Scalability: Microservices allow for greater scalability compared to monolithic architectures. Services can be scaled independently based on demand, leading to better resource utilization and cost efficiency.

Flexibility: Microservices are more flexible and adaptable

to changing requirements. New features can bedeveloped and deployed independently without affecting the rest of the application.

Faster Development Cycles: Microservices enable faster development cycles by allowing teams to work ondifferent services concurrently. This leads to faster time-to-market and better agility.

Fault Isolation: Microservices are designed to be resilient to failures. If one service goes down, it does notimpact the rest of the application, leading to better fault isolation.

Improved Maintainability: Microservices are easier to maintain compared to monolithic architectures. Each service is self-contained and can be updated or replaced without affecting the rest of the application.

Challenges of Microservices

While there are many benefits to using microservices, there are also several challenges that organizations may face when adopting this architecture style:

Complexity: Microservices introduce a level of complexity that may be challenging for some organizations tomanage. Coordinating communication between services, managing data consistency, and monitoring the health of the system can be complex tasks.

Distributed Systems: Microservices are inherently distributed, which can lead to issues such as network latency, communication failures, and security vulnerabilities.

Data Management: Managing data in a microservices architecture can be challenging, as each service has its own database. Ensuring data consistency and integrity across services can be a complex task.

Testing: Testing microservices can be challenging due to the distributed nature of the architecture. Ensuring that all services work together seamlessly and that changes to one service do not impact others can be a complex task.

Best Practices for Microservices

To successfully implement a microservices architecture, it is important to follow best practices:

Design for Failure: Microservices are designed to be resilient to failures. It is important to design services with failure in mind, and to implement strategies such as circuit breakers, retries, and timeouts to handle failures gracefully.

Use API Gateways: API gateways can help to centralize communication between services and provide a single entry point for clients. This can help to simplify service discovery and make it easier to manage communication between services.

Implement Service Discovery: Service discovery is crucial in a microservices architecture to enable services to find and communicate with each other. Implementing a service registry or using a service mesh can help to automate service discovery and make it easier to manage communication between services.

Monitor and Measure: Monitoring is crucial in a microservices architecture to ensure the health and performance of the system. Implementing monitoring tools and metrics can help to identify issues early and ensure that the system is running smoothly.

Automate Deployment: Automating deployment processes can help to streamline the release cycle and ensure that changes are deployed consistently and reliably. Using tools such as Docker and Kubernetes can help to automate deployment and scaling of microservices.

Microservices architecture offers many benefits, including scalability, flexibility, and faster development cycles. By understanding the key characteristics of microservices and following best practices

Designing APIs for Microservices

Designing APIs for microservices is a crucial aspect of building a successful and efficient microservices architecture. APIs act as the communication layer between different microservices, allowing them to interact with each other and exchange data seamlessly. In this article, we will explore the best practices for designing APIs for microservices, including defining clear boundaries, choosing the right communication protocols, and ensuring scalability and flexibility.

Defining Clear Boundaries

One of the key principles of microservices architecture is defining clear boundaries between different microservices. This includes defining the responsibilities of each microservice and the data that they are allowed to access and manipulate. When designing APIs for microservices, it is important to adhere to these boundaries and ensure that each API endpoint is responsible for a specific functionality or data set.

One way to achieve clear boundaries is to use a domain-driven design approach when designing APIs for microservices. This involves defining a domain model for each microservice, which includes the entities, aggregates, and value objects that are relevant to that microservice. By following a domain-driven design approach, you can ensure that each microservice has a well-defined scope and clear boundaries, making it easier to design APIs that align with the microservice's responsibilities.

269

Choosing the Right Communication Protocols

Another important aspect of designing APIs for microservices is choosing the right communication protocols. The communication protocol determines how different microservices will interact with each other and exchangedata. There are several communication protocols that are commonly used in microservices architecture, including REST, gRPC, and messaging protocols like Kafka and RabbitMQ.

When choosing a communication protocol for your microservices APIs, it is important to consider factors such as performance, scalability, and ease of use. REST is a popular choice for designing APIs for microservices, as it is simple to implement and widely supported. However, REST may not be the best choice for high-performance applications that require low latency and high throughput.

On the other hand, gRPC is a modern communication protocol that is designed for high-performance, low-latency communication between microservices. gRPC uses Protocol Buffers as its serialization format, which allows for efficient data exchange between microservices. gRPC also supports features like bidirectional streaming and authentication, making it a powerful choice for designing APIs for microservices.

Messaging protocols like Kafka and RabbitMQ are another option for designing APIs for microservices. These protocols allow for asynchronous communication between microservices, which can help improve scalability andfault tolerance. However, messaging protocols can be more complex to implement and may require additional infrastructure to support.

Ensuring Scalability and Flexibility

Scalability and flexibility are crucial considerations when designing APIs for microservices. Microservices architecture is designed to be scalable, allowing you to easily add or remove microservices as your application grows. When designing APIs for microservices, it is important to ensure that your APIs are flexible enough to accommodate changes in your application's architecture.

One way to ensure scalability and flexibility is to design your APIs using a versioning strategy. By versioning your APIs, you can introduce changes to your API endpoints without breaking existing clients. This allows you to iterate on your APIs and add new features without disrupting the functionality of your existing microservices.

Another way to ensure scalability and flexibility is to design your APIs with a focus on loose coupling. Loose coupling means that each microservice is independent and does not rely on the internal implementation details of other microservices. By designing your APIs with loose coupling in mind, you can easily swap out or update individual microservices without affecting the overall functionality of your application.

Designing APIs for microservices is a complex and challenging task, but by following best practices like

271

defining clear boundaries, choosing the right communication protocols, and ensuring scalability and flexibility, you can build a robust and efficient microservices architecture.

By designing APIs that align with the responsibilities of each microservice, you can create a cohesive and well-structured architecture that is easy to maintain and scale. Remember to consider factors like performance, scalability, and flexibility when designing APIs for microservices, and always strive to adhere to best practices and industry standards.

Conclusion

Congratulations on reaching the end of *Python for Web APIs: Design, Build, and Integrate RESTful APIs*! You've just unlocked the keys to mastering the art of creating seamless and efficient web communication. Throughout this journey, we've delved into the core principles of RESTful API design, explored the intricacies of Python for building robust APIs, and uncovered the secrets to integrating these APIs with various web services.

From understanding the fundamentals of REST architecture to implementing authentication and ensuring scalability, you've acquired the tools and knowledge necessary to transform your ideas into powerful, interactive web solutions. We've tackled real-world challenges and explored best practices that will not only enhance your technical skills but also elevate your problem-solving abilities in the realm of web development.

As you step into the world of API creation with newfound expertise, remember that this book is more than just a guide—it's a launchpad for your innovation. Whether you're crafting APIs for a small project or scaling solutions for enterprise-level applications, the principles and techniques you've learned here will serve as your foundation.

So, go forth with confidence and creativity! Harness the

power of Python to build APIs that connect, engage, and drive the future of web technology. The possibilities are boundless, and your journey has just begun. Embrace the challenges, celebrate your successes, and continue to push the boundaries of what's possible in the world of web APIs.

Thank you for joining me on this exciting adventure. Here's to your continued growth and to the incredible APIs you'll create!

Biography

Derek Randolph is a visionary in the world of web technology, renowned for his expertise in designing, building, and integrating RESTful APIs using Python. With a passion for web development and a knack for crafting elegant solutions, Derek has dedicated his career to pushing the boundaries of what's possible in the digital realm.

With years of hands-on experience and a deep understanding of both the technical and creative aspects of web applications, Derek has become a sought-after mentor and speaker in the tech community. His journey began with a fascination for programming, evolving into a profound expertise in Python and a drive to create seamless and efficient web experiences.

Outside of his professional endeavors, Derek is an avid hacker and coding enthusiast, always exploring new technologies and experimenting with innovative ideas. His love for programming is matched only by his enthusiasm for teaching others, and he takes great joy in guiding aspiring developers through the complexities of web APIs and application design.

When he's not immersed in code, you might find Derek exploring the latest trends in technology, contributing to open-source projects, or engaging in creative problem-solving challenges. His curiosity and dedication make him a true pioneer in the field, inspiring others to embrace the possibilities of technology and to never stop learning.

Derek's commitment to excellence and his vibrant approach to web development shine through in his work, making him a standout figure in the tech world. With this ebook, he shares his wealth of knowledge and passion, inviting readers to embark on their own journey of creating innovative and impactful web solutions.

Glossary: Python for Web APIs

Python is a versatile programming language that is widely used for developing web APIs. In this glossary, we will explore some of the key terms and concepts related to Python for web APIs.

API (Application Programming Interface): An API is a set of rules and protocols that allows different software applications to communicate with each other. In the context of web development, an API is typically used to define the methods and data formats that applications can use to interact with each other.

REST (Representational State Transfer): REST is a set of architectural principles for designing web APIs. RESTful APIs use standard HTTP methods (such as GET, POST, PUT, and DELETE) to perform operations on resources. These APIs are designed to be stateless, meaning that each request from a client contains all the information needed to process the request.

JSON (JavaScript Object Notation): JSON is a lightweight data interchange format that is commonly used in web APIs. JSON is easy for humans to read and write, and it is also easy for machines to parse and generate. JSON data is typically represented as key-value pairs, similar to Python dictionaries.

XML (Extensible Markup Language): XML is another data interchange format that is commonly used in web APIs.

XML is more verbose than JSON, but it is also more flexible and extensible. XML data is represented using tags, similar to HTML.

HTTP (Hypertext Transfer Protocol): HTTP is the protocol used for transferring data over the web. HTTP defines a set of request methods (such as GET, POST, PUT, and DELETE) that clients can use to interact with web servers. Web APIs typically use HTTP to send and receive data.

URL (Uniform Resource Locator): A URL is a string of characters that identifies a web resource. URLs are used to specify the location of resources on the web, such as web pages, images, and API endpoints. URLs consist of several components, including the protocol (such as http:// or https://), the domain name, and the path to the resource.

Endpoint: An endpoint is a specific URL within a web API that corresponds to a particular resource or action. Clients can send requests to endpoints to retrieve data, create new resources, update existing resources, or delete resources. Each endpoint in a web API is typically associated with one or more HTTP methods.

Request: A request is a message sent by a client to a server, typically using the HTTP protocol. Requests contain information about the desired action (such as retrieving data or updating a resource) and any data that needs to be sent to the server. Requests may also include headers, which provide additional information about the request.

Response: A response is a message sent by a server to a client in response to a request. Responses contain the requested data, along with metadata such as status codes and headers. Responses may also include error messages or other information related to the request.

Status Code: A status code is a three-digit number that is returned by a server in response to a client request. Status codes indicate the outcome of the request, such as whether the request was successful, failed, or redirected. Common status codes include 200 (OK), 404 (Not Found), and 500 (Internal Server Error).

Authentication: Authentication is the process of verifying the identity of a client before allowing access to a web API. Authentication mechanisms are used to prevent unauthorized access to sensitive data or resources. Common authentication methods include API keys, OAuth tokens, and username/password authentication.

Authorization: Authorization is the process of determining what actions a client is allowed to perform within a web API. Authorization mechanisms are used to enforce access control policies and restrict the actions that clients can take. Authorization is typically based on the client's identity, roles, and permissions.

Token: A token is a piece of data that is used to authenticate and authorize a client within a web API. Tokens are typically generated by the server and provided to the client as part of the authentication process. Tokens may be short-lived or long-lived, depending on the security requirements of the API.

Rate Limiting: Rate limiting is a technique used to restrict the number of requests that a client can send to a webAPI within a certain period of time. Rate limiting helps to prevent abuse of the API and ensure fair usage by all clients. Rate limits are typically enforced based on the client's IP address or authentication token.

Pagination: Pagination is a technique used to divide large sets of data into smaller pages for easier navigation. Pagination is commonly used in web APIs to limit the amount of data returned in each response. Clients can request specific pages of data using query parameters, such as page number and page size.

Serialization: Serialization is the process of converting data into a format that can be easily transmitted over a network. In the context of web APIs, serialization is used to convert Python objects into JSON or XML data that can be sent in HTTP requests and responses. Serialization may also involve converting data between different formats or structures.

www.ingramcontent.com/pod-product-compliance
Lightning Source LLC
LaVergne TN
LVHW051437050326
832903LV00030BD/3128